Leadership for Safe Schools

A Community-Based Approach

Raymond L. Calabrese

The Scarecrow Press, Inc.
Scarecrow Education
Lanham, Maryland, and London
2000

SCARECROW PRESS, INC.

Published in the United States of America
by Scarecrow Press, Inc.
4720 Boston Way, Lanham, Maryland 20706
www.scarecrowpress.com

4 Pleydell Gardens, Folkestone
Kent CT20 2DN, England

British Library Cataloguing in Publication Information Available

Library of Congress Cataloging-in-Publication Data

Calabrese, Raymond L., 1942–
    Leadership for safe schools : a community-based approach / Raymond L. Calabrese.
        p. cm.
    Includes bibliographical references (p.) and index.
    ISBN 0-8108-3886-9 (alk. paper) — ISBN 0-8108-3898-2 (pbk. : alk. paper)
    1. School violence—United States—Prevention. 2. Community and school—United
States. 3. Educational leadership—United States. I. Title.

LB3013.3 .C32 2000
371.7'82—dc21

                                                              00-044546

∞™ The paper used in this publication meets the minimum requirements of
American National Standard for Information Sciences—Permanence of
Paper for Printed Library Materials, ANSI/NISO Z39.48–1992.
Manufactured in the United States of America.

This book is dedicated to my best friend and wife, Barb; my parents, Annie and Louis Calabrese, who taught me to believe in my ideas and myself; and my daughters, Prudence, Catherine, Angela, Michelle, and Christine.

Contents

Preface

School is one of the safest places a child can be. Yet, every day, 13 students on average are suspended, expelled or arrested for bringing a firearm to school. Since the tragedy at Columbine High School, more than 5,000 bomb threats have been made at schools. More than 1 million acts of violence, from fistfights to murders to suicides, occur every year.[1]

Every community desires safe schools. What is the difference between communities that have safe schools and those struggling with school-related violence? Leadership is the difference. Leaders believe that the community is the resource for solving problems. The school leader invests in human potential, energy, and spirit of renewal. As the leader, the principal is the catalyst for the community to construct a safe school environment.

John W. Gardner, leadership expert and former cabinet member under President Lyndon Johnson, states:

The consideration leaders must never forget is that the key to renewal is the release of human energy and talent. We have all seen those gleaming projections of the society of the future that feature an endless array of technological marvels and never mention human talent and energy. It is as though the technology invented itself. Similarly one sees projections of wonderfully efficient new administrative structures with very little thought given to the men and women who will have to make these structures work and redesign them if they don't work. We must be equally skilled in nurturing men and women who have the capacity to see the problems and the spirit to solve them. The capacity of a system to renew itself continuously is dependent in part on the capacity for renewal of the men and women in the system. The structures and processes don't redesign themselves.[2]

The school leader, following Gardner's advice, recognizes teachers, parents, students, and community members as important resources. These human resources collaboratively have the experience, intelligence, and skill to create a safe school environment. The school leader needs to know how to effectively use these resources. This book provides the school leader with a process to collaboratively construct a safe school plan.

The school leader following the process presented in this book focuses on full community participation. He or she intuitively recognizes the general concern the public has with school safety. A *USA Today*/CNN/Gallup Poll indicates that 70 percent of parents are concerned about their child's safety in school.[3] These parents want to be involved with the school principal in creating a safe school environment. This process brings citizens and educators together to take responsibility for creating a sustainable safe school environment.

Leadership for Safe Schools: A Community-Based Approach complements the movement toward democratization and partnership building within schools. This book shows the school leader how to form partnerships to develop a safe school plan. It provides the knowledge, skills, and direction to empower the school leader and the school community to develop a safe school environment. Together, community members and educators can discover the political, social, and educational benefits of collaboration.

The school leader, after reading this book, learns how to facilitate a dynamic team-driven process to construct a safe school environment. The school leader increases leverage with faculty, students, and the community. Members of the school and community will recognize that the principal's leadership results in higher morale, a healthier environment, and greater collaboration.

This book follows the advice of Peter Senge, author of *The Fifth Discipline,* who states, "The 'stake' I wanted to put into the ground would establish systems thinking, mental models, personal mastery, shared vision, and team learning and dialogue as inescapable elements in building learning organizations."[4]

The school leader has the capacity to re-create the school as a learning organization. As a learning organization, the school leader facilitates learning among teachers, students, parents, and community members. These community members learn that they are partners, working on the same side of the table, sharing similar values and goals. This book provides the leadership strategies to accomplish this task. Are you ready to exercise your leadership in guiding your community in the construction of a safe school environment? Chapter 1 is waiting for you.

I have used the personal pronouns *he* and *she* to avoid awkwardness in reading. I also present many examples to illustrate essential points. The names and places are all fictional, but each story is real.

It is impossible to write a book like this without a great deal of assistance. I would like to acknowledge the help of many individuals. Of special note, I want to thank my friend and wife Barb, whose support for this project sustained me. Many people at Scarecrow Press have helped the writing process and encouraged my efforts. I thank Kate Kelly, acquisitions editor, for exploring and supporting the idea of a publishing a book that shows principals how to lead community-driven efforts to construct a safe school environment. I also extend thanks to Christine Ambrose, production editor, and Laura Larson, copyeditor. Every author needs an editor who shares the vision and dream of the author: Dr. Tom Koerner, editorial director for Scarecrow Education, a trusted friend, colleague, and champion for this project, is that person. Finally, I thank my colleagues, Dr. Sally Zepeda at the University of Georgia, who provided critical comments and suggestions, and Dr. John Kelly, superintendent of schools at Boerne, Texas, for providing insights on coalition building.

NOTES

1. Bruce Rosenstein, Scott Bowles, and Hilary Wasson, "Threat of Violence throughout School Year," *USA Today*, 14 April 2000, 13(A).

2. John W. Gardner, "There Is More Than a Ray of Hope for America's Future: Rebuilding America's Sense of Community." <http://www.newciv.org/qual/americancommunity.html> (21 April 2000).

3. *USA Today*/CNN/Gallup Poll, "Parents' and Public's Reaction to Columbine," *USA Today*, 14 April 2000, 7(A).

4. Peter Senge, *The Fifth Discipline: The Art and Practice of the Learning Organization* (New York: Doubleday, 1990), x.

CHAPTER ONE

Planning for Safe Schools

Safe schools are possible in America. A safe school is the desire of the school community. Parents want their children to be safe; teachers want to teach without fear of threat of reprisal; administrators want to concentrate on creating and maintaining an achievement-focused environment; and students want a supportive and stimulating environment. A safe school fulfills these desires through a collaborative planning process that includes the members of the school community. This planning process assimilates the unique needs of the school and community into a focused strategic safe school plan. This chapter discusses the preparation process that precedes the strategic planning for a safe school.

In this chapter, you will

- understand how to integrate the three cornerstones of a safe school environment into your planning,
- understand the planning essentials for constructing a strategic safe school proposal,
- use information to gain leverage in the planning process,
- sharpen your group processing skills, and
- select an effective safe school planning team.

Traditionally, school discipline focused on student classroom behavior. Now, discipline encompasses the emotional and physical safety of the school community. School administrators continually search for new programs and strategies to cope with this evolving challenge. They know that creating a safe school environment is important to students, teachers, and parents. Yet, with all the attention given to creating a safe school environment, many school administrators see safe schools as an enigma rather than something tangible. They feel powerless in a turbulent world where violence erupts unexpectedly. Appropriate reaction to these events, for many administrators, is a necessary coping skill.

Other school administrators choose to be proactive. These administrators control their destiny. They are unwilling to allow events to determine their fate. Safe school environments do exist—in the inner city, suburban enclaves, and rural areas—but they receive little attention. The news media instead diverts attention to sensational and catastrophic cases. Safe schools are not newsworthy. The administrators, teachers, students, and parents associated with the safe school operate in anonymity. As a result, seldom are their practices replicated. A school in one district has a safe environment, and a school two blocks away with a similar population has an unsafe environment. These are similar schools with dissimilar results. It is simplistic to believe a single factor made one school safe and the other unsafe. It is unfair to single out students, teachers, parents, school administrators, or the socioeconomic status of the community for existing conditions. A safe school environment results from collaboration among administrators, teachers, parents, and students.

Collaboration produces four significant benefits:

1. It fosters communication among groups.
2. It links people to a common cause.
3. It focuses on constructive activities.
4. It creates a spirit of community.

Effective strategies and practices emerge from collaborative, community-building efforts. People realize they have the power to transform their environment through involvement in constructive action.

The collaboration process affords the first visible evidence of developing a safe school strategy. Collaboration produces a sound learning environment that includes physical and emotional safety evolving from the school's unique context. Successful school administrators view safe school strategies as unique to their school. They know that external solutions, although technologically sound and substantive, are not applicable to all situations. Stewart Purkey states that it does not matter what strategy the school adapts as long as they adapt it to their specific circumstances and maintain a high level of consistency in its application.[1]

THREE CORNERSTONES OF CONSTRUCTING A SAFE SCHOOL ENVIRONMENT

Figure 1.1 depicts the three cornerstones of a safe school environment:

- Integrity
- Learning and teaching
- Culture and values

Integrity

Integrity is the integration of values with behavior and actions resulting in positive outcomes for the person and society. James Kouzes and Barry Posner, leadership experts, state:

> [Integrity is] a personal creed [that] gives you a point of reference for navigating the sometimes stormy seas of organizational life. Without a set of such beliefs, our lives are rudderless, leaving us without control of our destiny. A credo to guide you prevents confusion on the journey. Personal integrity is essential to believability.[2]

Figure 1.1   The Three Cornerstones of a Safe School Environment

Integrity links the organization's external and internal moral and ethical reference points to the people within and external to the organization. It integrates moral and ethical reference points. External groups look at the school organization and see one voice, one mission, one vision, and one set of integrated values and actions. Integrity aligns school's values and purpose with those of the community.

Learning and Teaching

The second cornerstone, learning and teaching, is essential to instructional leadership. Students attend school to "develop new knowledge through a process of active construction. They actively mediate it by trying to make sense of it and relate it to what they already know about the topic."[3] The teacher, through the craft of teaching, facilitates this process.

We can apply the same learning and teaching process used in English, mathematics, or science to discipline. Discipline is an important safe school component with a specific knowledge base. Teachers communicate this knowledge base to students rather than seeing it as an administration issue. Discipline is a part of the teacher's role when the teacher integrates the student's social growth into the framework of teaching and learning. Charles and Mary Wolfgang believe that discipline is an act of teaching and learning in which the learner acquires personal restraints and becomes more cooperative.[4] Social growth includes learning problem solving, decision making, conflict mediation, negotiations, and identification of values such as respect, civility, and trust.

Central to the integration of discipline into teaching and learning is the belief that the act of teaching has a significant moral impact on the learner. According to Alan Ornstein, "How a person develops morally is partially, if not predominantly, based on the way he or she interacts with family, schools, and society—more precisely, on the roles and responsibilities he or she learns and deems important based on contact with people who are considered important."[5] As a result, the student grows intellectually, socially, and morally. The teacher reinforces the student's intellectual, social, and moral growth. In essence, every place where a student and teacher interact, a potential learning environment exists. When the teacher integrates moral development into academic areas, the relationship of the teacher and student becomes the means of constructing the classroom learning environment.

The teacher has the responsibility for cultivating this relationship. The teacher, as the primary deliverer of instruction, links intellectual pursuits to the student's experience. By moving into the student's world, the teacher creates a psychological link embracing physical, spiritual, intellectual, and emotional components. Teachers who integrate moral development into their classroom operate from sound psychological learning perspectives. These teachers understand that well-prepared classes that integrate the students' context maintain the students' interest and provide the basis for moral and social formation. This integrated approach links the psychological components of learning and teaching.

Culture and Values

The school and the community use culture and values to create a sense of mutuality. Schools that sustain a collaborative culture unleash the members' creative energies and skills. Collaboration as a core component fosters a professional learning community that supports planning and creative problem solving.[6]

A community's culture considers customs and symbols. Customs and symbols include community ceremonies, storytelling of the community's history, pageants, celebration of local heroes, and award banquets. At a deeper level, the culture expresses how the community communicates, understands time, and defines relationships and primary roles within the context of families. Like the community, each school has a set of values. These values drive relationships between teacher and student, teacher and parent, and administrator and teacher. They establish the type of community that exists within a school.

Values differ from community to community and school to school. Three important values, however, of any democratic organization are mutual respect, civility, and communication (see Figure 1.2 for the interaction among these three values). Schools, at their best, are democratic institutions and reflect these values. John Dewey said, "Democracy is more than a form of government; it is primarily a mode of associated living, of conjoining communicated experience. The extension in space of the number of individuals who participate in an interest so that each has to refer his own action to that of others, and to consider the actions of others to give point and direction to his own."[7]

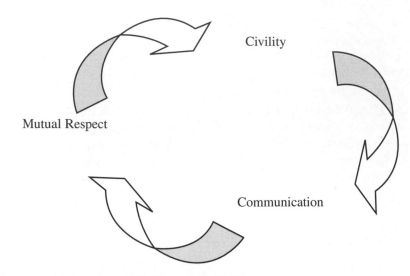

Civility

Mutual Respect

Communication

Figure 1.2   Interaction of the Three Critical Values

Mutual Respect

Successful organizations, whether social, family, or business, operate with mutual respect. School leaders teach mutual respect through modeling. When the principal respects teachers, teachers respect students. When teachers respect students, students respect teachers. Mutual respect is at the core of all school relationships.

Civility

Civility frames the way that members of a democratic organization engage in debate. Guy and Heidi Burgess, codirectors of the Conflict Research Consortium at the University of Colorado, state, "Civility requires that contending parties make an honest and continuing effort to understand the views and reasoning of their opponents. Civility also requires that the public issues be addressed by a process that is fair in both appearance and fact."[8] Civility is a social vehicle that allows people to collaborate in mature democratic organizations. Many students come to school without appropriate models of civility. School becomes the place to provide opportunities for students to learn that civility is the appropriate way to interact in social settings.

Communication

Psychologist Virginia Satir states, "Communication covers the whole range of ways people pass information back and forth: it includes the information they give and receive, the ways that information is used, and how people make meaning out of this information."[9] Effective communication demands honesty. Honesty encourages expression without the threat of repercussion or recrimination. Honest communication facilitates understanding and breaks down the barriers of fear, hostility, and confusion. Communication serves as the basis for building inclusive communities.

The members of the Harvard Negotiating Team state, "Communication is never an easy thing, even between people who have an enormous background of shared values and experience. It is not surprising, then, to find poor communication between people who do not know each other well and who may feel hostile and suspicious of one another."[10]

The three cornerstones of a safe school environment are the foundation for sound teaching and high student achievement. When these cornerstones are in place, the members of the school community feel empowered to handle any emergency and to develop long-term solutions to problems within the context of the school community.

PLANNING FOR A SAFE SCHOOL ENVIRONMENT

A safe schools strategy requires effective planning. Efficient and insightful planning is an important factor in the implementation of a strategy and a well-developed, skillfully executed plan. Planning requires the reflective examination of the school community's social, cultural, political, and economic context. Effective planning integrates community participation into the development of a safe school strategy.

Participation is a critical part of the planning process. Partnerships for Preventing Violence indicate that lack of community participation in schools increases the chance for violence, whereas communities that promote participation in decision making in neighborhood schools create safe schools and neighborhoods.[11] Thus, broad participation in planning is a community-building, empowering process. The more community members participate, the more widespread the acceptance and commitment to the planning process.

Planning and Culture

The cultural context refers to the community's ideas, customs, symbols, and values, which influence what happens in the school. Both dominant and subdominant cultures exist within a community. A dominant culture's customs, symbols, and values are present in everyday experience. However, involvement of all cultures is crucial to the planning process. Use the following chart as a guideline for identifying the dominant and subdominant cultures in your community:

School–Community Cultures

Dominant culture: Example: Latino	*Leader:* Mario Sanchez, chairperson, community action group
Subdominant culture 1: Example: Jewish	*Leader:* Rabbi Thomas Fisher, Temple-Beth-El
Subdominant culture 2: Example: Anglo (rural white farmers)	*Leader:* Michael Smith, chairperson, Farmer's Co-op

Each school is an expression of the multiple cultures within its community. The students carry their family's culture to school each day. The family culture helps students to understand their world. When the student's cultural viewpoint differs from the majority cultural viewpoint, conflict is likely to occur. For example, José Rameriz, a twelfth grade Latino student, was taught at home that he must be respected at all times. When a teacher belittles José in front of his peers, Jose feels humiliated and responds by walking out of the class. He experiences inner conflict when a disparity between the cultural values of the school and his cultural values exists. If José chooses to obey his parents, he violates the teacher's code and is subject to punishment. If he chooses to obey the teacher, he violates his parents' code.

The incongruence between culture systems exists at many levels. A Dallas newspaper reported that a school scheduled a meaningful academic experience during the Jewish holidays. The Jewish community complained to the school leaders; however, the event went on as scheduled. Few Jewish students attended this event; thus, hostility developed between the Jewish community and the school administration. The Jewish students were confused because they felt that their teachers wanted them to attend the event, but their parents wanted them to honor their Jewish heritage. The confusion felt by the Jewish students is known as *cognitive dissonance*. An understanding of cultural diversity within the school community and the gifts of each culture promote collaboration and cooperation.

Planning and Values

Different cultures espouse different educational values. Reconciling these differences creates a sense of community among members. When school administrators ignore differences and assume that all people view the world through the same lens, conflict occurs. For example, the *Houston Chronicle* reported:

> Fearful that a gang called the Bloods would terrorize the town and her students, too, the principal of Round Rock High School decided one day to ban the color red. So for three weeks this month, students who showed up in scarlet were asked to change clothes or were sent to in-school suspension. Some shrugged. Others rolled their eyes. One girl, whose wardrobe was dominated by red, cried. A group of vocal parents grew irate.[12]

The principal had to rescind her ban. However, if the principal involves the community in meaningful dialogue, she averts the problem. As part of an effective planning process, school administrators and their team identify the primary and secondary values associated with cultures in the school community. Use the following chart as a guideline for listing the primary and secondary values associated with the dominant and subdominant cultures in your community:

School–Community Cultural Values

Name of Culture	Primary Value	Secondary Value
Dominant culture		
Subdominant culture 1		
Subdominant culture 2		

Planning and the Political Environment

Effective planning identifies the community's political environment. This environment includes teacher unions, special interest groups, and other political groups. Identifying these groups and their aspirations allows the school leader to determine each group's motivation. Understanding the motivation frees the school leader to construct a political umbrella embracing each group's aspirations. Use the following chart as a guideline for identifying political groups and their political agenda and aspirations.

Identification of Political Groups

Political Groups	Political Agenda	Political Aspirations

Planning and Interdependence

A democratic society relies on the interdependence within the school and community. Administrators, teachers, parents, and students need each other and must work together for the common good. When these groups unselfishly work together, interdependence is seen at its best. Robert Bellah in *Habits of the Heart* states:

> [W]e have never been, and still are not, a collection of private individuals who, except for a conscious contract to create a minimal government, have nothing in common. Our lives make sense in a thousand ways, most of which we are unaware of, because of traditions that are centuries, if not millennia, old. It is these traditions that help us to know that it does make a difference who we are and how we treat one another.[13]

The foundation of a safe school environment begins with a process that relies on the cooperation of the community including the participation, aspirations, and values of its members.

Planning and the Economic Context

The economic context determines the resources available to develop an effective safe school strategy. The economic context also reflects the community's values. For example, in blue-collar communities where the parents earn an hourly wage, the parents cannot afford to take time off to meet with teachers during the school day, whereas in white-collar communities, many parents can arrange their work schedule to meet with school officials during the school day. What one community sees as a necessity another community may view as a frill. The school leader must be cognizant of these differences. This is especially true when the school leader lives in a more affluent community than the community where his or her school is located. Planning has to take into consideration the economic condition of the school community.

USING INFORMATION TO GAIN LEVERAGE IN THE PLANNING PROCESS

Information is the power tool of the twenty-first century. The more information school leaders have, the more power that is available to them. Effective school leaders recognize that information drives the planning process, facilitates collaboration, reflects on actual experience, shapes opinion, and influence attitudes. The school leader collects and disseminates balanced information. This approach maintains the school leader's credibility. Members of the school community realize that the school leader is not using information to manipulate but as a source that affects attitudes.

Consider the following data:[14]

- Eighty-two percent of young people under eighteen have working mothers.
- Sixty percent of children under six have mothers working outside the home.
- Sociologists predict that the majority of the children in school will live with a single parent before they graduate.
- Grandparents are becoming an increasing factor in raising children.
- Nearly one-fourth of all children in the United States are born to a single mother.
- Nearly one-fourth of all children under the age of eighteen are living below the poverty level.
- More than 80 percent of all prison inmates are high school dropouts.

This information describes the at-risk nature of American children. It provides an understanding to the motivation underlying student behavior. With this type of information, those involved in the planning process can understand the relationship of adolescents to society and discover previously hidden problems. Information such as this can help to identify the origin of symptoms of dysfunctional behavior.

Gaining Leverage

The right information provides the means to accomplish your purpose—or, to put it another way, it provides leverage. School leaders use information to gain leverage and create the power for action. The greater the leverage provided by information, the more impetus that exists to create a proactive environment. The school leader uses leverage as a source of motivation to influence the actions of other people. Leverage is equal to the benefit minus the cost associated with the benefit. When the benefit outweighs the cost, leverage acts as a motivational factor. The greater the gap that school community members recognize between benefits and cost, the greater the leverage. When no gap exists, there is no leverage. For example, a teacher uses the leverage of attendance on a field trip as a means of motivating students to complete a paper on time. She informs the students that those who submit their term papers on the assigned date are eligible to participate in a field trip to New York City. The leverage the teacher is using is the trip to a new and exciting place. The benefit from the students' point of view is the opportunity to go to New York City. Since the cost of writing the paper is far less than the benefit they receive, the students attend class and write their papers. The teacher uses leverage as an effective instructional tool. Similarly, the school leader uses leverage by relating, for instance, that 82 percent of U.S. prisoners have a history of being high school dropouts.

SHARPEN YOUR GROUP PROCESSING SKILLS

Selecting and facilitating a team are critical components in the planning process. The Prevention Institute believes that the community is the source for any action and ideas to resolve the issues of school violence. They recommend Larry Cohen's eight-step guide for bringing a team or coalition together:

1. Determining needs and objectives.
2. Recruiting the right members.
3. Linking the group's actions to the member's strengths.
4. Inviting appropriate players to participate.
5. Mapping resources and needs.
6. Devising the group's structure.
7. Planning to ensure the group's success.
8. Continuous evaluation of outcomes.[15]

The school leader needs group facilitation skills, the ability to gain consensus, and knowledge of how to build a cooperative team before putting a team together to start the planning process.

Facilitation is a basic group process tool. "The facilitative leader shares responsibility with the participants for the group's development."[16] The more the school leader practices facilitation, the more effective she becomes as a facilitator. The school leader's primary task in facilitating the group process is to create a safe environment. The leader creates a safe environment when she clearly defines parameters within which the group communicates. These parameters include identifying the time frame for the group's existence, how the group reaches agreement on decisions, and identification of unacceptable tactics. Groups have a high degree of freedom when they operate with a clear set of parameters. This safe environment reduces anxiety and potential conflicts.

Once the school leader establishes a safe environment, she can focus on group leadership characteristics. These characteristics include the ability to work effectively with people, a positive attitude, the ability to create a climate of confidence, flexibility, patience, skill to develop consensus, and motivational skills. The leader applies these characteristics to the group process. As a result, the group becomes a place for generative action where the fermentation of ideas and constructive dialogue lead to strategies directly applicable to constructing a safe school environment.

Gaining Consensus

There is an array of opinions regarding consensus. Some think that consensus means that all participants have to agree before the group proceeds, while others believe that consensus is the will of the majority after taking into account the voices of minority opinions. In general, consensus requires that all members of the group agree to support the decision even if the decision does not represent the outcome the individual member desired. William Ouchi, management expert, states that groups achieve consensus when members believe that others understand their point of view, that they understand all other points of view, and that all decisions resulted from a fair and democratic process.[17]

Full participation and trust among members are fundamental to gaining consensus. With little trust, we gain little agreement. The following guidelines provided by the Washington State University Cooperative Extension Service facilitate consensus building:[18]

- Everyone contributes to the discussion.
- Each participant shares opinions and has his opinion respected and included in the process.

- Differences are helpful and contribute to a synergistic effect.
- Members agree to disagree and are willing, after full discussion, to test the decision.
- Each member has sufficient time to express himself before making a final decision; people feel safe that they will have the necessary time to express themselves and their ideas.
- All participants take ownership of the final decision.

Using this process, all dissenting opinions are part of the process. The dissenting members have the opportunity to move from dissent to offering constructive alternatives. Every person has a chance and a responsibility to offer solutions. This is democratic participation. When the leader follows these guidelines, a consensus generally occurs because the leader involves everyone.

The use of these guidelines will achieve consensus with minimal disruption. Sally Zepeda, education professor at the University of Georgia, states, "This upfront work, described in the preceding paragraphs, saves time in the end and the process minimizes politics and focuses the energy of the group into a more proactive stance for addressing the issues and finding solutions."[19]

Building a Cooperative Team

The effective leader knows that building a cooperative team is an important part of the planning process. According to Kouzes and Posner, "Your capacity to strengthen and empower others begins with the degree of power that you hold—your connection to lines of supply, information, and support. Only leaders who feel powerful will delegate, reward talent, and build a team composed of people powerful in their own right."[20] The school leader draws from the members of the school community to form the safe school planning team. She analyzes the prospective team member's potential contribution, ability to communicate effectively with constituents, and willingness to make a long-term commitment while building a history to work constructively toward consensus.

She begins by identifying the prospective members and their skills. The composition of the team is important to its success. The school leader takes into account political, collegial, and other characteristics in selecting members. Consideration of these factors allows the school leader to create a balanced team.

She checks the member's background, reputation within the school and community, types of skills, abilities, and knowledge, ability to work with people, and motivation.[21] The school community instinctively trusts these people. These people will be responsible for the flow of information to the school community and for constructive feedback. Use the following chart to identify potential team members:

Identification of Prospective Team Members

Name of Member	Skills	Respect	Positive Force	Rating (1 = low; 10 = high)
		Y N	Y N	
		Y N	Y N	
		Y N	Y N	
		Y N	Y N	
		Y N	Y N	
		Y N	Y N	
		Y N	Y N	
		Y N	Y N	

Note: Respect refers to whether the prospective member has the community's respect; Y = yes, N = no. *Force* refers to the prospective member's potential to be a positive contributing member to the team; Y = positive, N = negative.

Foundation Values

Foundation values are essential to broad-based acceptance of the planning outcome. These values reflect membership in a democratic society. Values include trust, democratic participation, inclusion, and leadership. Members act in each other's best interest when they trust each other. William James stated:

> A social organism of any sort whatever, large or small, is what it is because each member proceeds to his own duty with a trust that the other members will simultaneously do theirs. A government, an army, a commercial system, a ship, a college, an athletic team, all exist on this condition without which not only is nothing achieved, but nothing is even attempted.[22]

Democratic participation encourages the involvement of all school community members in the process. The team represents their voice, aspirations, and desires. Democratic participation builds and sustains the sense of interdependence necessary for this project. Inclusion affords participation at direct and indirect levels. The astute school leader recognizes that effective teams are necessarily small. Even though he works with a small team, the school leader and his team create numerous channels for open communication with the rest of the school community. The school leader understands that leadership is situational; he continuously adapts his leadership style to the context, skills demanded, and outcomes sought by the team. He knows that effective groups rotate the informal leadership as issues change. As a result, he identifies each member's leadership potential and encourages him or her to lead.

Alignment of the Task with Safe School Criteria

A knowledge base already exists for designing a safe school. The team only has to take the knowledge base and adapt it to the needs of the community. When aware of safe school criteria, team members use it as a guide for discussion. The criteria become benchmarks for the development of effective strategy. The following checklists (see page 17) showing teacher and administrator characteristics of effective schooling practices provide a format for a planning analysis of the presence or lack of evidence of their existence in the school.[23]

THE LEADER'S CHALLENGE

The primary challenge of the leader is to encourage, nurture, and support team members. The leader helps members overcome periods of discouragement, disagreement, and discord. Leadership in a democratic society implies trust in people. Leadership requires investment of time and an investment in people. When a leader commits to the process, members recognize the leader's high level of commitment. This high level of commitment, in turn, builds self-esteem, enhances confidence, and creates a sense of inclusion.

SUMMARY

Developing an effective safe school strategy is an important agenda for the school leader. An effective safe school strategy can improve the lives of the students, teachers, administrators, and parents. The team the school leader selects has an opportunity to lay the groundwork for a unique environment to influence the students' intellectual, social, and moral experiences. This strategy, aligned with effective school characteristics, takes into account the community's cultural context, values, political environment, economic conditions, and sense of interdependence. The planning team is cocreating, codeveloping, and collaborating to develop a unique formula for the most effective and efficient outcomes.

Checklist for Teacher Characteristics to Create/Sustain a Safe School Environment	
Teacher Responsibilities and Duties in a Safe School Environment	*Exists* ✓
Teachers form instructional groups that fit students' academic and affective needs.	
Teachers make efficient use of learning time.	
Teachers establish smooth, efficient classroom routines.	
Teachers set clear standards for classroom behavior and apply them fairly and consistently.	
Teachers carefully orient students to lessons.	
Teachers provide clear and focused instruction.	
Teachers routinely provide feedback to students and reinforcement regarding their learning process.	
Teachers review and teach as necessary to help all students master learning material.	
Teachers use validated strategies to help build students' critical and creative thinking skills.	
Teachers use effective questioning techniques to build basic and higher-level skills.	
Teachers integrate workplace readiness skills into content area instruction.	
Teachers hold high expectations for student learning.	
Teachers provide incentives, recognition, and rewards to promote excellence.	
Teachers interact with students in positive, caring ways.	
Teachers give high-needs students the extra time and instruction they need to succeed.	
Teachers support the social and academic resiliency of high-needs students.	
Teachers promote respect and empathy among students of different socioeconomic and cultural backgrounds.	
Teachers monitor student progress closely.	
Teachers make use of alternative assessments as well as traditional tests.	

Checklist for Administrator Characteristics in a Safe School Environment	
Administrator Responsibilities and Duties in a Safe School Environment	*Exists* ✓
Administrators and teachers base curriculum planning on clear goals and objectives.	
Administrators and teachers integrate the curriculum as appropriate.	
Administrators and teachers provide computer technology for instructional support and workplace simulation.	
Administrators and teachers include workplace preparation among school goals.	
A school-based management team makes many of the decisions regarding school operations.	
Administrators and teachers organize students to promote effective instruction.	
Administrators and teachers assure that school time is used for learning.	
Administrators and teachers establish and enforce clear, consistent discipline policies.	
Administrators and teachers provide a pleasant physical environment for teaching and learning.	
Leaders undertake school-restructuring efforts as needed to attain agreed-on goals for students.	
Strong leadership guides the instructional program.	
Administrators and other leaders continually strive to improve instructional effectiveness.	
Administrators and other leaders engage staff in professional development and collegial learning activities.	
Administrators communicate high expectations for teacher performance.	
Administrators and other leaders provide incentives, recognition, and rewards to build strong staff motivation.	
Administrators and teachers communicate high expectations to students and recognize excellent performance on a schoolwide basis.	
Administrators and teachers provide programs and support to help high-needs students achieve school success.	
Administrators and teachers work to achieve equity in learning opportunities and outcomes.	
Administrators and teachers work to establish and maintain positive relationships among people of different socioeconomic and cultural backgrounds.	
Administrators and teachers provide multicultural education activities as an integral part of school life.	
Administrators and teachers provide challenging academic content and English language skills for language minority students.	
Administrators and other building leaders monitor student learning progress.	
Administrators and other building leaders develop and use alternative assessments.	

Administrators and teachers identify dropout-prone students and implement activities to keep them in school.

Administrators and teachers use validated practices for tobacco, alcohol, and drug prevention.

School leaders and the staff collaborate with community agencies to support families with urgent health and/or social service needs.

Administrators and teachers involve parents and community members in supporting the instructional program.

Administrators and teachers involve parents and community members in school governance.

Putting It Together: Advancing with Vigilance	✓
Have you identified each culture in your school community? Have you identified the values, symbols, and other important aspects of the cultures in your community? Have you identified the skills that you need on the planning team? Have you identified a pool of potential candidates for the planning team? Have you selected team members based on skills, positive contribution, and the respect by school community members? Have you spoken to your school community about the opportunity that they have to participate in this process? Have you asked members to make a long-term commitment to this process?	

NOTES

1. Stewart Purkey, "A Cultural-Change Approach to School Discipline," in *School Discipline Strategies*, ed. Oliver Moles (Albany: SUNY Press, 1990), 63–76.

2. James Kouzes and Barry Posner, *The Leadership Challenge* (San Francisco: Jossey-Bass, 1987), 301.

3. Thomas Good and Jeri Brophy, *Looking in Classrooms* (New York: HarperCollins, 1997), 398.

4. Charles Wolfgang and Mary Wolfgang, *The Three Faces of Discipline for Early Childhood* (Boston: Allyn & Bacon, 1995).

5. Alan Ornstein, *Strategies for Effective Teaching* (New York: HarperCollins, 1990), 22–23.

6. Kent Peterson, "The Importance of Collaborative Cultures," Wisconsin Center for Education Research (WCER), School of Education, University of Wisconsin, Madison, *Reform Talk* 10 (1997).

7. John Dewey, *Democracy in Action* (New York: Free Press, 1966), 101.

8. Guy Burgess and Heidi Burgess, "The Meaning of Civility," unpublished manuscript, Conflict Research Consortium, University of Colorado (1998), <http://www.colorado.edu/conflict/civility.htm> (29 March 2000).

9. Virginia Satir, *The New Peoplemaking* (Mountain View, Calif.: Science and Behavior Books, 1988), 52.

10. Roger Fisher, William Ury, and Bruce Patton, *Getting to Yes* (New York: Penguin, 1983), 32.

11. Kevin P. Dwyer and David Osher, "Early Warning, a Timely Response: A Guide to Safe Schools," unpublished manuscript, Center for Effective Collaboration and Practice of the American Institutes for Research in collaboration with the National Association of School Psychologists (1999), <http://cecp.air.org/guide/files/2.htm> (11 April 2000).

12. Polly Ross Hughes, "Principal Isn't Red-Faced about Color Ban," *Houston Chronicle*, 22 October 1998, 1N.

13. Robert N. Bellah, *Habits of the Heart* (Berkeley: University of California Press, 1985), 282.

14. Eric P. Hartwig and Gary M. Ruesch, *Discipline in the School* (Horsham, Pa.: LARP, 1994).

15. Larry Cohen, Nancy Baer, and Pam Satterwhite, "Developing Effective Coalitions: An Eight Step Guide," ed. Kelly O'Keefe, the Prevention Institute, Berkeley, California <http://www.preventioninstitute.org/eightstep.html> (11 April 2000).

16. Richard Nelson-Jones, *Group Leadership: A Training Approach* (Pacific Grove, Calif.: Brooks/Cole, 1992), 19–20.

17. William Ouchi, *Theory Z* (New York: Avon, 1981).

18. "WSU Cooperative Extension Family Community Leadership and 'Consensus' in Community Leadership Leader's Guide," adapted from *Making Decisions by Consensus,* Washington State University Cooperative Extension in Spokane County, <http://www.spokane-county.wsu.edu/family/consen.htm> (29 March 2000).

19. Sally Zepeda, University of Georgia, Athens, Georgia. Written correspondence (April, 2000).

20. Kouzes and Posner, *The Leadership Challenge,* 175.

21. William Sahlman, "How to Write a Great Business Plan," *Harvard Business Review* (July–August 1997).

22. William James, *The Will to Believe* (New York: Dover, 1897), 24.

23. Kathleen Cotton, "Effective Schooling Practices: A Research Synthesis 1995 Update," Northwest Regional Educational Laboratory (1995; material taken directly from this source), <http://www.nwrel.org/scpd/esp/esp95toc.html> (29 March 2000).

CHAPTER TWO

Shared Values: The Foundation to Commitment

This chapter explains how to identify critical core values and how to generate school and community commitment to these values. Values are the inner expression of external actions. Core values drive an effective safe school strategy. A safe school strategy becomes operational through each member's commitment to the strategy. A value-driven strategy produces widespread commitment by bringing a high degree of specificity, direction, and strength to the team's purpose.

In this chapter, you will

- identify personal and collective values,
- identify critical shared values,
- use shared values to create a heightened sense of community,
- develop team commitment, and
- increase team members' sense of integrity.

THE LEADER'S ROLE IN DEVELOPING SHARED VALUES

A *value* is an axiom, criterion, or attribute considered worthwhile or desirable either by an individual or by a team. As such, values serve as the standard for judging and directing our lives. Selecting values that propel us in the right direction is difficult in cultural contexts with a myriad of competing values. These values, often in opposition, compete for primacy in our personal and professional lives. Some people, for example, claim that values are relative, while others argue that there is a primacy among values. How are leaders and followers to know which values are the most beneficial? The fact that values are both personal and communal further complicates this issue. Values are personal in the sense that each individual lives by a set of self-selected values. They are communal in the sense that societies operate on the basis of shared values.

The successful leader and her organization hold fast to a primacy of values. She identifies mutually beneficial values that promote the health of the organization and its members. These values are mutually beneficial in that they complement the values held by the members of her organization. The values of her organization and those held by its members operate synergistically in effective organizational settings. She manifests these values in her actions. Her values are on display for each member of the organization and community.

Values provide leaders and their organizations with a moral compass. Powerful leaders know that "[a]uthentic values are those by which life can be lived, which can form a people that produces great deeds and thoughts."[1] Organizations that specialize in training leaders focus first on identifying core values and imparting these values to the people they are training. For example, the U.S. Air Force in "The Little Blue Book" states, "The Core Values are much more than minimum standards. They remind us what it takes to get the mission done. They inspire us to do our very best at all times. They are the common bond among all comrades in arms, and they are the glue that unifies the force and ties us to the great warriors and public servants of the past."[2]

All viable institutions discover identifying core values essential to their mission. The U.S. Air Force, for example, identifies three primary core values: integrity, service before self, and excellence. The U.S. Navy considers its core values as honor, courage, and commitment. Walt Disney regards imagination and wholesomeness as its core values. The Sony Corporation cites the promotion of the Japanese national culture, attaining global status, being a trailblazer, doing the unattainable, and encouraging personal ability and inventiveness. The Nordstrom Corporation identifies service to the consumer, hard work, personal productivity, satisfaction, and distinction in reputation. Proctor and Gamble believes product excellence is its core value.[3] In addition, Conservative Judaism refers to its core values as the sacred cluster composed of seven essential tenets.[4] These institutions, public and private, religious and social, all share the common belief that people and organizations need essential values. The core values of these institutions have a sense of timelessness. They do not change from day to day. They have an innate relevancy that transcends momentary acceptance or disputation.

The organization's core values govern decisions, behaviors, and attitudes. These core values provide the organization with a sense of identity by shaping the institution's boundaries. With a sense of identity, members understand their mission. When people have difficult decisions to make, they simply refer to their core values to serve as a compass. Researchers James Kouzes and Barry Posner state, "The research makes clear that shared values do make a difference to organizational and personal vitality and that values form the bedrock of an organization's corporate culture. Unique values make for unique corporate cultures."[5] In one sense, our values are unique. In another sense, our values link members of the organization. Commonly shared core values have a linking property that makes it easy to carry out the organization's mission. According to Stephen Covey, "Proactive people can carry their weather with them. Whether it rains or shines, it makes no difference to them. They are value driven; and if their value is to produce good quality work, it isn't a function whether the weather is conducive to it or not."[6]

The leader helps team members to identify constructive and positive core values. Educational researchers Kent Peterson and Terrence Deal state:

> School leaders from every level are key to shaping school culture. Principals communicate core values in the everyday work. Teachers reinforce values in their actions and words. Parents bolster spirit when they visit school, participate in governance, and celebrate successes. Leaders uncover and articulate core values, looking for those that buttress what is best for students and support student-centered professionalism.[7]

The school community's core values empower faculty, students, parents, and administrators by guiding diverse teams toward a common destiny.

Identifying shared core values is a difficult but necessary task. The identification of shared core values is a challenge because most people operate from a zero-sum paradigm. *Zero-sum* is a term used by decision-making researchers to explain why people fail to see alternatives. In effect, many people have an inclination to limit their alternatives to two choices and negate all others. As a result, they select a single strategy and then rule out the potential value of all other strategies. Operating from a zero-sum paradigm leads potentially to undermining actions that cause greater divisiveness rather than building community. The astute school leader does not operate from a zero-sum paradigm; rather, he shapes his school team to discover shared core values by avoiding potential sabotaging myths and embracing inclusive dialogue.

SABOTAGING MYTHS

There are two sabotaging myths driven by assumptions held by the school leader.

Myth 1: The Team Leader Imposes His Values as the Team's Values

The leader believes that the team should adopt his values, not realizing that people resist having values imposed on them. The members of the team feel as strongly about their values as the leader does about his values. The imposition of values is a faulty strategy. It often has a temporary positive effect when organization members are desperate for help. When members are desperate for help, they are willing to try anything. They know that their survival is at stake. Once they become secure, they begin to question the leader's imposed values. Successful school leaders avoid this pitfall by working with team members to identify shared values.

Myth 2: The Leader Assumes That Everyone in the Same Work Environment Shares the Same Values

The lack of overt opposition or resistance often results in school leaders believing that everyone agrees with the leadership's proposal. The school leader may assume that all members desire to follow a politically correct path. Such assumptions can be false. When the school leader pursues these assumptions, she creates a situation where the phenomenon known as *groupthink* emerges. Groupthink occurs in a situation where all members of the team feel that they have to support the proposed course of action. The effective school leader, recognizing her responsibility to involve all people in determining the shared values of the organization, constantly involves members in determining shared values. Successful school leaders avoid this pitfall by consistently checking for understanding and agreement.

IDENTIFYING CORE VALUES

The process to identify and integrate shared core values proceeds through four stages:

1. The identification of personal values
2. The identification of shared values
3. The identification of personal and organizational boundaries
4. The integration of shared values

The Identification of Personal Values

The first step in identifying shared core values is to help organizational members identify personal core values. Personal core values significantly influence each member's life. Once members identify their core values, they can construct paths for their core values to align with the values held by other team members. The school leader uses many different methods to draw out core values. In one situation where I facilitated the discovery of shared core values, I asked each person to share a story of a teacher who made the difference in his or her life. We focused on an experiential event, not on the discussion of core values. Each member expressed his or her experiential event as shared stories of a teacher who had a dramatic impact on his or her life. As each person shared his or her story, the members of the team began to sense that person's values. At the conclusion of this process as a result of each person sharing his or her story, the team intuitively understood the values shared. The team recognized they shared the core values of compassion, integrity, and high standards.

The following story stimulates thinking and identification of personal core values.

Imagine a plank one foot wide, three inches thick, and twenty feet long. It sits on the ground and separates you from me. Imagine that I have $20 in my hand, and all you have to do to gain that $20 is to walk across the plank. There are no strings attached; all you have to do is to walk across the plank. My guess is that you will walk across that plank and collect the $20. I now move the plank and set it on two poles five feet above the ground. The plank is still one foot wide and three inches thick. Instead of $20, however, I hold a cashier's check for $1,000. All you have to do is walk across the plank and collect the check. Will you walk across the plank for the $1,000? I now convert the plank into an I-beam made of the strongest steel in the world (an I-beam is a heavy metal beam shaped like an *I*). The width of the I-beam is two feet. It connects the Twin Towers in New York City. People below look like insects as they scurry along the sidewalks. I increase the reward for

walking across the I-beam to $100,000. Imagine, before you begin, that
the wind is blowing at thirty to forty miles per hour and that there is a
slight rain coming in off the water in New York Harbor. I want to encourage people to cross the I-beam, so I increase the reward to
$1,000,000—and the speed of the wind increases to sixty miles per
hour. Will you cross the I-beam and risk your life for $1,000,000? Now
imagine that I am holding the person you love most in your life over the
edge of one of the Twin Towers. Your loved one will be dropped if you
do not cross the I-beam. Will you cross the I-beam?[8]

This activity seldom fails; people who refuse to cross the I-beam for
$1,000,000 will cross the I-beam to rescue someone they love. When you
identify the reason for crossing the I-beam, you identify your primary values. This activity is powerful because each person can identify with the
instant reaction of someone who says, "I'm coming across." They understand that this process moved them beyond the superficial identification
of values to a substantive identification of core values. These are personal
values that, when violated, will cause cognitive dissonance. The violation
of other values may cause temporary pain, but they will not cause great
personal, psychological, and emotional distress.

It is important that each team member identify the values vital to his
personal well-being. When members align their values, they create a sense
of inclusion. For example, a team member stated, "When I did the exercise, one of the critical values that I identified was my family. I used the
identification of this value as a source of motivation in responding to the
members of my school community. In this way, I carried my core values
with me at home and at work. As a result, when I went back to my school,
I treated everyone as a member of my family—what a difference it made
for me as principal."

IDENTIFYING SHARED VALUES

The identification of shared values begins with the identification of a personal value system (PVS). A PVS has both intrinsic and extrinsic values.
Extrinsic values are highly valued objects, ideas, and people external to
the self. A person, for example, may say that she values her work or house.
Here, work and house are extrinsic values. *Intrinsic values* are concepts,
feelings, or ideas that are part of a person's being. Other people only know
these values through interpreting a person's actions. For example, respect

is an intrinsic value because it is an internal representation of how a person wants to be treated. Members recognize respect in the actions of the person who operates with respect as an internal value. As team members define a personal value system, they gradually realize that their actions represent internal and external values. The combination of these values identifies their PVS.

Identifying Extrinsic and Intrinsic Values

The school leader can use the following process to assist team members in identifying extrinsic and intrinsic values.

Give each team member ten small rocks (or alternate objects). Ask team members to identify ten intrinsic values they feel are important and attach each value to a rock (e.g., rock 10 represents caring). Slowly and deliberately, ask the team members to reflect on what each rock represents. After a period of reflection, have members identify a value to discard. They then discard a rock. Continue this process of discarding values (rocks) until team members reach that set of values (rocks) that they cannot discard. These remaining values represent their set of intrinsic values.

This process can also help identify extrinsic values. When the team completes this process, they have the components of their PVS. Each external and internal value receives a priority ranking. The values that have the highest priority are value-drivers. A *value-driver* is each person's primary motivating value. Value-drivers propel the actions that each person takes during the course of the day.

LINKING SHARED VALUES TO A SAFE SCHOOL STRATEGIC PLAN

The school leader integrates three essential components when linking shared values to a strategic plan:

- Awareness
- Behaviors
- Words

Awareness is a personal or organizational mindfulness of feelings, motivations, actions, objects, and events. It is awareness of internal and external activity. Awareness is reflective questioning that assesses the consistency of behaviors with a shared PVS. Awareness of the consistency of alignment between behaviors and shared values provides integrity. Awareness enables team members to challenge actions that undermine the team's integrity since the actions are not consistent with the team's values.

Behavior is the activity or response of a person or a team to external or internal stimuli. It is a visible action to a perceived response. For example, when we are at a busy city intersection, we stop (behavior) and become aware of traffic. The light changes, and we walk (behavior in response to the light change) across the intersection. A behavior also results from internal stimuli. A teacher, for example, witnesses a sixth grade student pushing a first grade student. The teacher steps in between the students (behavior based on an internal sense of justice or fairness) to prevent the older child from harming the younger child.

Our behaviors link our values to the strategies we develop. When the behaviors of administrators, teachers, parents, and students emanate from identified shared core values, the behaviors become the external representation of the safe school strategy. When a direct correlation exists between behavior and value-drivers, the safe school strategy demonstrates a sense of integrity. When all behaviors are value driven, consistency between the team's identity and the team's actions emerges. For example, if one of the school's intrinsic values is respect, a teacher publicly berating a student because the student did not take a book to class is not an action consistent with this value.

Words are the primary vehicles to communicate the values inherent in behavior. Words express our thoughts through a medium that others understand. Words, however, are the source of problems when a word's meaning is not consistent between the speaker and listener. The following example demonstrates this dilemma.

A teacher says to a student, "One more word and I am sending you to the principal."

The student says, "What?"

The teacher responds by sending the student to the office. The student tells the principal that she was asking for clarification of the teacher's remarks. The effective school leader understands what is happening in this context. He knows that words are powerful. They can hurt or heal. They build or destroy. This perception allows the school leader to deal effectively with this situation.

The school leader, recognizing the power of words, uses appropriate wording to influence the school's value system. He carefully chooses words that represent critical school values. He knows that when he uses a word frequently, it becomes common currency among members of the organization. If personal integrity is part of the school's PVS, for example, then the school leader and teachers integrate the word *integrity* into the common vocabulary. The school leader can use statements such as these:

"We can maintain our integrity by. . . ."
"It is important for our school's integrity. . . ."
"This action is consistent with values and therefore sustains our whole sense of integrity."

The effective school leader uses value words in agendas, verbal or written correspondence, or daily discourse. Using the precise words on a consistent basis, the school leader discovers that other members of her organization use the same vocabulary. The school leader's awareness and appropriate use of language are critical to the sharing of a PVS.

It is through awareness, behavior, and words that others come to understand shared core values. Lynne McFarland and her coauthors, in *Twenty-first Century Leadership: Dialogues with 100 Top Leaders,* tell us (words) that the values mentioned most by these top leaders were integrity, honesty, openness, trust, teamwork, caring, openness to change, respect, innovation, a can-do attitude, and balance in life.[9] These words, used by America's top hundred leaders, communicate important values. How do these words and values match with the values your team has selected?

LINKING VALUES TO SAFE SCHOOL STRATEGIES THROUGH COMMUNICATION

Effective communication is an art form. Only those people who understand this art form are consistently effective communicators. One way that the effective communicator expresses this art form is in the understanding of the appropriate time and place to communicate. The effective communicator knows that competition (e.g., noise and other distractions) deflects attention from effective communication. As a result,

the effective communicator distinguishes between appropriate and inappropriate times to communicate. An appropriate time to communicate
has the following three components:

- Appropriateness of time
- Attention of audience
- Appropriateness of context

The appropriate time to communicate is when there is maximum re-
ceptivity by the listeners to the speaker's communication. The president
of the United States does not communicate to the nation during a national
emergency at four A.M., for example. The president, if possible, wants to
be on television during prime viewing hours to communicate with the
public. Effective leaders avoid inappropriate communication times. Inappropriate communication times include the presence of confusion, lack of
attention, and high levels of emotions. Each of these distracts the speaker
and listener from fully sending and receiving the communication. Distractions, when they overwhelm the meaning of the message, result in the
misinterpretation of the message. The true message never arrives. Consequently, poor communicators spend more time resending the message.

The effective communicator determines whether the audience is receptive to hear the message. This does not mean that the message is always pleasing to the audience. The message may make the audience un-
comfortable. If those communicating the message, however, have the
attention of the audience, they have a better chance for successful communication. For example, John List, high school principal, suspended a
student from school. The student and the student's parents were angry.
The parents felt that the suspension was unjustified. John realized that
any discussion related to the school's metaphor (see chapter 3) or expectations for the student would be empty words to the parents. John
chose to wait to share the school's safe school philosophy and values
until the student returned with her parents. He reasoned that this was a
more appropriate time to communicate value-drivers since the student
and parents had time to reflect on the incident. He knew that all parties
would be more receptive to his message.

It is up to the communicator to identify the appropriateness of context.
Appropriateness of context is the environment where the audience is most
receptive to the message. In general, school leaders and teachers assume
that the school is the most appropriate context to convey a message. It

may be beneficial to the school leader and teachers to choose a different context to communicate their message. Community churches, local meeting halls, and homes of students provide appropriate contexts for communication with the community.

USING SYMBOLIC EVENTS AS A MEANS OF COMMUNICATING VALUES

Symbols, according to Paul Ricoeur, are

> those expressions carrying a double sense which traditional cultures have grafted onto the naming of the "elements" of the cosmos (fire, water, wind, earth, etc.) of its "dimensions" (height and depth, etc.). These double-sense expressions are themselves hierarchically ordered into the most universal symbols, then those that belong to one particular culture, and, finally, those that are the creation of a particular thinker, even of just one work. In this last case, the symbol merges into living metaphor.[10]

Symbols are ways that one generation communicates cultural values to the next generation. They are part of a cultural system to keep values represented by the symbol fresh in the minds of the members of the culture. Members attach meaning to the symbol. It is common to see people fight over symbols without reflecting on the symbol's meaning. The American flag, for instance, is an important symbol to many people. Burning or desecrating the flag raises strong emotions. Hence, the symbol relates closely to emotion or feeling rather than to rational thought.

Joseph Campbell, the famed anthropologist, states:

> Dr. John Perry has characterized the living mythological symbol as an "affect image." It is an image that hits one where it counts. It is not addressed first to the brain, to be there interpreted and appreciated. On the contrary, if that is where it has to be read, the symbol is already dead. An "affect image" talks directly to the feeling system and immediately elicits a response, after which the brain may come along with its interesting comments. There is some kind of throb of resonance within, responding to the image shown without, like the answer of a musical string to another equally tuned. And so it is that when the vital symbols of any given social team evoke in all its members responses of this kind, a sort of magical accord unites them as one spiritual organism, functioning through members who, though separate in space, are yet one in belong and belief.[11]

Each school has events that act as symbols to communicate its own and its community's values. These symbols link the school to the community's deepest held values. Some symbolic events traditionally held in many schools include graduation, pep rallies, awards ceremonies, and National Honor Society induction nights. Let's consider some examples of how different schools have used symbols to communicate shared core values.

Denton High School uses the concept of family as their primary value-driver. At each commencement, the school welcomes the community as part of the Denton High School family. Each year the administration communicates to the community and student body how graduates remain members of the school's family. Denton High School has created a sense of interconnectedness with its community. Its graduations are well attended by intergeneration members. It does not matter to community members whether they have a relative graduating from school; attendance at graduation is a community event.

Laughton Middle School created a symbolic event by having an annual night to honor students who made the honor roll for three consecutive marking periods. Annually, the school leader and teachers reward students expressing the values of industry and achievement. The student and his or her extended family received a free dinner at the award ceremony. These events symbolically communicate the school's value-drivers to the community.

The school leader, as the moral and transformational leader of the school, takes personal responsibility to convey the school's shared values. Management and leadership expert Peter Vaill states, "Leadership is the articulation of new values and the energetic presentation of them to those whose actions are affected by them."[12] If the school leader's actions match the school's values, the school community will readily adopt those values. If the school leader fails to provide values matched by actions, others assume the leadership role and provide a competitive set of values. Lori Smith, principal at Carver Middle School, was unable to connect her values to her actions. Consequently, a small team of teachers with pessimistic attitudes took control of faculty meetings and determined the entire culture of the school. Jean Danforth, who replaced Lori, acted with integrity. Each of Jean's behaviors expressed her values. Jean quickly created a learning and team-driven environment at Carver Middle School. Value-driven leadership influences and shapes the actions of others and the culture of an organization.

ESTABLISHING BOUNDARIES

Value-driven leaders and value-driven organizations have a clear sense of boundaries. A clear set of boundaries allows a person or organization to have a well-defined set of internal and external expectations. According to leadership expert Thomas Sergiovanni, when members of the organization share values, commitment and bonding among members takes place.[13] Shared values provide boundaries that are essential to effective leadership and organizational identity.

Unmistakable boundaries contribute to personal and organizational effectiveness. Vaill states, "High performing systems are very conscious of their boundaries, and so are individuals and teams who are on the 'outside.'"[14] This sense of awareness of boundaries results from a well-defined set of values and consistent value-driven actions. These boundaries enable the team to focus on the task of developing a strategic safe school plan. The school leader facilitates the process of establishing boundaries by focusing on four boundary-discovering components:

1. Clarifying responsibility
2. Eliminating role confusion
3. Defining relationships
4. Creating commitment

Clarifying Responsibility

When the school leader clarifies responsibility, her teachers and students have clearly delineated lines of responsibility. Many at-risk schools exhibit a high level of ambiguity related to delineated lines of responsibility. This lack of understanding regarding role responsibility generates a sense of confusion, hair-splitting accusations, and defensiveness among teachers and administrators. It undermines morale and efforts to develop a sense of community. In environments where delineated lines of responsibility are present, morale soars and cooperation is a norm.

Delineating lines of responsibility is a complex task because the school organization has many different overlapping roles. The gestalt of the actions associated with these roles contributes to an effective safe school environment. When the gestalt of role responsibility is high, the school environment will be correspondingly more effective. Increased effectiveness occurs when each team member identifies his role and takes responsibility within that role for creating and maintaining a safe school environment. Table 2.1 lists roles found in many schools. The school leader can use this table to identify similar roles found in her school and to associate responsibility with the role.

Table 2.1 Roles and Role Responsibilities

List of School Roles	*Responsibility of the Role*
Role of the principal	
Role of the assistant principal	
Role of the teacher	
Role of the counselor	
Role of the nurse	
Role of the secretary	
Role of the custodian	
Role of the student	
Role of the parent	
Role of the teacher's aide	
Role of police officers	
Role of student mentors	
Role of student teachers	
Role of coaches	

Eliminating Role Confusion

The school leader eliminates role confusion by identifying expectations for each role. Working with her team, the school leader develops a set of expectations for each role. A major source of role confusion is the inability to differentiate between authentic and counterfeit roles. A *counterfeit role* is one in which the party in question ignores the responsibilities associated with his authentic role and assumes the responsibilities associated with another role. Consequently, fulfillment of responsibilities for either role is lacking.

One example of the use of a counterfeit role occurs when a teacher ignores the disrupting behavior of the child in her classroom. Rather than confront the problem, the teacher takes on the responsibilities of the counselor and tries to understand the child. During this process, the child's behavior becomes increasingly intolerant and the learning environment less stable. Conversely, playing an authentic role the teacher understands her associated responsibilities. She takes her role seriously, maintaining a high level of role responsibility. The authentic teacher does not ignore the child's behavior. The authentic teacher challenges the student's disruptive behavior and works with administrators, counselors, and parents to maintain an effective learning environment. The authentic teacher does not have role confusion.

Misplaced role expectations are another cause of role confusion. Misplaced role expectations occur when the person fulfilling the role fails to act consistently with the image others have of the role. We refer to the images that others have of the role as *role expectations*. Often, role expectations drive the actions that we take to our roles. For example, a parent would not go into a school and expect the principal to be dressed in a bathing suit or to a school board meeting and expect the superintendent to be wearing a baseball uniform. These role expectations are the primary operating standard that the school community uses to determine whether the person in the role is effective.

In effective schools, there is a close alignment between role expectations and role responsibilities. This alignment contributes to consistent behavior and value-driven decisions.

Role expectations allow each person to evaluate his performance against the standard of expectations set for the role. This in turn contributes to increased performance because each person precisely recognizes role expectations. Ironically, few schools work to identify roles or role expectations. Effective school leaders understand the importance of delineating clear roles and establishing standard setting role expectations.

Defining Relationships

Effective school leaders work with their teams to define working relationships. They understand that competent relationship skills are the foundation of effective organizations. Four factors are essential in establishing effective working relationships:

- Openness
- Honesty
- Nonjudgment
- Context understanding

Openness means that each party in the relationship has the co~~~~ence to self-disclose and become vulnerable in the working relationship. To the degree that a person trusts the other in the relationship, the relationship sustains openness. The willingness to embrace openness becomes difficult when members receive neither the time nor the encouragement to develop trusting relationships. This is frequently an unrecognized systemic issue in which members attribute lack of openness to personal faults rather than to the organization's structure. In most organizational settings, focus on work detracts from the effort needed to develop effective relationships. Openness is possible, but it requires recognizing the unity in diversity and overcoming structural and personal barriers to openness.

Honesty is synonymous with *honor* and *integrity*. Each of these words describes the quality of being ethical in principle and action. Honesty means that a person is guileless, fair in dealing with others, and not deceitful in his relationships. Effective relationships are grounded in honesty when both individuals express their feelings, suggest personal points of view that may be in complete opposition, and do not try to control the other person in the relationship.

Effective relationships are also *nonjudgmental*. Each party in these relationships evaluates facts without referring to stereotypes, biases, or other referencing criteria. When the school leader allows such factors to interpret facts, she judges without understanding the context within which the facts occur. Effective school leaders and teachers apply judgments only to events. A child or adolescent who misbehaves in school is not bad. Rather, the event was inappropriate. This is good psychology.

All organizations exist within a dynamic context. Effective working relationships occur within this dynamic context. A dynamic context is one where boundaries constantly shift, relationships end and begin, complexity exists, and change is a constant factor. MIT management professor Peter Senge, in speaking about systems thinking, states:

> Today, systems thinking is needed more than ever because we are becoming overwhelmed by complexity. Perhaps for the first time in history, humankind has the capacity to create far more information than anyone can absorb, to foster far greater interdependency than anyone can manage, and to accelerate change far faster than anyone's ability to keep pace.[15]

To build effective relationships in a complex environment, the school leader understands the dynamic context of the school community. Karen Smith, principal of Ellison High School, wanted to form more effective relationships with her teachers. Her first step was to ask them, "What is it like to be a teacher?" "What is it like to be in a classroom with thirty students?" "What is it like to be a teacher when a student threatens you?" "What is it like to be a teacher when parents confront you?" *Understanding the context* begins by collecting data from those who comprise the context. Karen began this process by obtaining information from her teachers. The school leader gathers this information by identifying the data related to the experience of members within the context.

The closer the team comes to defining relationships, the closer the team comes to identifying and establishing boundaries and an identity. The establishment of personal boundaries becomes a guideline for coaching and working with people. The coaching process used below is an effective tactic in implementing the safe school strategy.

Once boundaries exist with a corresponding set of expectations related to responsibility, role, and relationships, there is a set of benchmarks to mark progress and to assess accountability. The following dialogue between a principal and teacher shows how the principal coaches the teacher to become more effective in the area of classroom management by defining the teacher's role.

> **Principal:** Can you tell me how you have defined your role as teacher?
> **Teacher:** I really haven't thought about it.
> **Principal:** Let's see if we can define the role of teacher. Tell me what you believe the role of a teacher to be.
> **Teacher:** Well . . . the teacher should teach students, make sure that they understand, and prepare them for the next level of instruction.
> **Principal:** That sounds like a good beginning. Can you tell me about the classroom environment that a teacher should establish?

The teacher describes his image of an ideal classroom environment. During this process, the principal constantly frames and shapes the conversation until the teacher clearly defines his role. The principal, as coach and mentor, helps the teacher to establish boundaries for his teaching. The teacher and principal have collaboratively agreed to the conditions of work related to the teacher's context. The principal established an effective relationship with the teacher because of the principal's honesty and nonjudgmental approach.

Creating Commitment

The school leader generates commitment for the safe school plan by integrating shared values into the school organization and by using integrity as a benchmark value. School community members look for integrity in school leaders. They look for a direct match between the school leader's words and actions. The school leader's integrity is essential in building trusting relationships within the school community. The establishment of a commitment to integrity begins with the school leader. The greater the integrity of the school leader, the higher the trust the school leader receives from team members. When the school leader recognizes the critical nature of integrity, she adjusts her actions to match her words.

The school leader's commitment to acting with integrity builds broad-based trust and plants the seeds of integrity within each team member. Researchers have shown that publicly made commitments in the presence of meaningful persons have a greater chance of enduring. Psychologist Harry Dreher states:

> People strong in commitment find meaning and purpose in their work and relationships. They are capable of wholehearted involvement in their activities, and choose creative pursuits and relationships based on their potential meaningfulness. By contrast, people low in commitment lack meaning and purpose. They tend to be alienated from their work and/or relationships.[16]

It is important to use this psychological tool to secure team commitment to the strategy, process, each other, and the school community. The following activity deepens levels of commitment among members of the school community.

Commitment Activity

The school leader has members of her team list the commitments they made throughout their lives. A *commitment* is a decision to stay with a project until it is completed. One list can be for personal commitments, another for professional commitments. One person may list a commitment to getting a postgraduate degree. Another may list a commitment to caring for an elderly parent. Another person may list a commitment made to his spouse. Commitments mean staying power.

Each commitment listed by a team member has an inherent value associated with it. The value may be fidelity, self-respect, honesty, or friendship. The school leader asks each member to list the values associated with his commitments. As he lists his values, the school leader asks the team member to describe how these values enhanced the enduring quality of his commitments.

This activity creates a personal history of commitment for each member. It also allows members to see the linkage between their personal value system and the commitments that they kept. Team members will recognize that the commitments sustained related closely to the depth of values held by the members. Team members will recognize that they are more committed to what they value as opposed to something they do not value. For example, who would hire a coach who did not care about his players? How would players feel about this coach? Successful teachers, coaches, and school leaders have a strong commitment to their students, profession, and the school community. This process generates this sense of commitment.

Identification of Sustained Professional Commitment

Sustained commitment is a process-driven activity. This process begins by the school leader asking team members to identify one commitment they sustained. Once team members identify this commitment, the school leader asks team members to list the actions that they took to sustain and build that commitment. As each member identifies her ability to sustain commitment, she begins to link commitment to personal integrity. The identification of sustaining professional commitment becomes a source of strength for teachers, administrators, students, and parents. The school leader can transform this activity into a symbolic event by having team members recall the day they made the commitment to the team and to the development of the safe school strategy.

Integrity Check

The school leader sustains integrity by periodically conducting an integrity check. An *integrity check* is the measurement of consistency between commitments made and commitments kept. The school leader conducts an integrity check by facilitating team consensus on future commitments. For example, one commitment could be to attend meetings. Another commitment might be to hold the length of meetings to a certain time limit. Another commitment may be to distribute minutes of team meetings to school members or have them posted in public places for the students to read. The school leader can maintain a large poster board on a wall that says "Integrity Check."

The level of integrity of any team or person increases with the filling of each commitment made by a person or team. Each commitment made and kept becomes a mark of integrity. The integrity check poster has one column listing commitments made and another column listing commitments kept. It is important that the school leader sustains awareness among team members of commitments.

Commitment Day

The school leader sustains the importance of commitment by establishing a commitment day. It is during this commitment day that each team member makes a commitment to the team, the process, and the implementation of the safe school plan. The school leader asks each member to state his level of commitment to the team and process. The school leader leads by making the first statement of commitment: "I am committed to working with this team, students, teachers, and parents in a democratic process to develop an effective safe school plan. Even in times of disagreement, I am committed to working through those disagreements to find common ground. I will support each member of this team, and I will stay with the process. I will support the plan that we develop and stick with the implementation of that plan to its successful conclusion."

SUMMARY

This chapter discusses how to identify critical core values essential to building an effective safe school strategy. Shared core values provide a structure that lays a strong foundation for the development of an effective safe school. Shared core values emerge through the identification of personal values and a personal value system (PVS). The foundation built through the identification of shared core values is critical at a personal, team, and organizational level. Without this foundation, individuals, teams, and organizations drift. Shared core values provide a clear sense of identity. Although each person's values are unique and based on experience, underlying values unite each member. The school leader seeks to capture unity in diversity.

It is possible to identify positive values that empower the organization and its members. In identifying values central to organizational identity, the school leader uses the analogy of crossing the I-beam. The school leader links the values identified by crossing the I-beam to effective safe school strategies and actions. The primary and most important values that members identify are value-drivers. Value-drivers are a major motivational component for transforming the school. Value-driven leadership speaks to the means of communicating these shared values. Communication is a verbal and action-oriented activity in which values are an essential focus. The school leader communicates values through symbols, meetings, events, and vocabulary. Connecting all values is the primary value of personal integrity. Integrity is the confluence of one's actions, words, and physical presentation; it is the primary way of interacting with members of the school community.

Putting It Together: Advancing with Vigilance	✓
Does everyone understand the power of personal and team values? Did everyone identify personal values? Did everyone identify a personal value system (PVS)? Did members identify extrinsic as well as intrinsic values? Did the team agree on shared values? Did the team communicate the shared values to school community members? Are the shared values a part of the school's vocabulary? Did the team identify school roles? Did the team set expectations for these roles? Is there an integrity check poster in your meeting room? Did the team schedule a Commitment Day?	

NOTES

1. Allan Bloom, *The Closing of the American Mind* (New York: Simon & Schuster, 1988), 35.

2. "United States Air Force Core Values," United States Air Force Home Page (1999), <http://www.usafa.af.mil/core-value/> (10 April 2000).

3. James Collins and Jerry I. Porras, "Building Your Company's Vision," *Harvard Business Review* 74, no. 5 (September–October 1996).

4. Ismar Schorsch, "The Sacred Cluster: The Core Values of Conservative Judaism," Jewish Theological Seminary (1997), <http://www.jtsa.edu/pubs/schorsch/core.html> (10 April 2000).

5. James Kouzes and Barry Posner, *The Leadership Challenge* (San Francisco: Jossey-Bass, 1987), 194–95.

6. Stephen Covey, *The 7 Habits of Highly Effective People: Powerful Lessons in Personal Change* (New York: Fireside, 1989), 71–72.

7. Kent Peterson and Terrance Deal, "How Leaders Influence the Culture of Schools," *Educational Leadership* 56, no. 1 (1998): 28–30.

8. This story was adapted from a story told on a set of audiotapes produced by the Franklin Organization in explaining the Franklin Planner.

9. Lynne J. McFarland, Larry E. Senn, and John R. Childress, *Twenty-first Century Leadership: Dialogues with 100 Top Leaders* (New York: Leadership Press, 1996).

10. Paul Ricoeur, "On Interpretation," in *Philosophy in France Today*, ed. Alan Montefiore (Cambridge: Cambridge University Press, 1983), 192.

11. Joseph Campbell, *Myths to Live By* (New York: Viking Penguin, 1972), 92.

12. Peter B. Vaill, *Managing as a Performing Art* (San Francisco: Jossey-Bass, 1991), 55.

13. Thomas J. Sergiovanni, "The Leadership Need for Quality Schools," in *Schooling for Tomorrow: Directing Reforms to Issues That Count*, ed. Thomas J. Sergiovanni and John H. Moore (Boston: Allyn & Bacon, 1990), 213–26.

14. Vaill, *Managing as a Performing*, 70.

15. Peter Senge, *The Fifth Discipline: The Art and Practice of the Learning Organization* (New York: Doubleday, 1990), 69.

16. Harry Dreher, *The Immune Power Personality* (New York: Penguin Team, 1995), 128.

CHAPTER THREE

Developing a Shared Vision

This chapter shows how to develop a shared vision by constructing communal meaning. There are many ways to construct communal meaning. One way is to use a metaphor to bring diverse groups together to discover a shared vision. *Metaphors* are a common linguistic construction in which team members use a mutually understood symbol or image to designate a shared vision. Applying this everyday figure of speech enables team members to establish a sense of community based on personal histories and directed toward developing a safe school plan.

In this chapter, you will

- understand how to develop a shared vision,
- learn how to use a metaphor to create a shared vision,
- understand how to use the concept of metaphor to build community,
- gain consensus on a commonly shared metaphor, and
- facilitate the discovery of constructive personal metaphors among team members.

VISION

All leaders speak of vision. Leaders know that a clear vision is central to effective leadership. Understanding and applying the concept of a shared vision is an important component in developing a safe school. According to the North Central Regional Educational Laboratory, a vision has five characteristics:

1. A vision generates a motivating mental picture of the future.
2. Deeply held values are the source of motivation to attain the vision.
3. A vision, although distant and somewhat ambiguous, is attainable.

4. A vision provides hope to those who hold the vision.
5. A vision becomes real the more it is communicated and sought.[1]

Vision is a frequently applied yet often misunderstood term. Thomas Sergiovanni states, "[A vision] must also reflect the hopes and dreams, the needs and interests, [and] the values and beliefs of everyone who has a stake in the school."[2] It is "the force which molds meaning for the people of an organization."[3] Vision is one of the building blocks of leadership. Without vision, a group, unit, or person wanders aimlessly. The person or group has no destination, no compelling reason for moving from their present position to another, and much different position.

> A vision is not a dream that is conjured up in an office while the principal contemplates the future. A vision is value driven and marks the distant goal through which progress is constantly measured. It is the beacon that allows the organization and its members to continually course correct as they develop a clearer orientation toward the vision.[4]

Imagine a wagon train heading west across the American plains during the 1800s. The wagon master and members of the wagon train have a vision of their destination. The vision of each member of the wagon train is different yet similar. For some, the vision is a new lease on life, a farm, or free land. Each person on the wagon train has a vision that forms a loose-tight coupling with the visions held by other members. Developing a shared vision is not easy; as Tom Peters states, "Developing a vision is a messy, artistic process."[5] The process of constructing a vision is difficult because of the importance of its shared nature.

Components of an Effective Vision

First, a vision relates to the community and its context. When the vision relates to the community's context, community members understand the relevancy of the vision. The vision's relevancy motivates the community members to participate in this process.

Second, members with a personal stake in the future of the organization develop the vision collaboratively. Since most members remain in the organization long after the leadership leaves, the members act as the organization's anchors.

Third, the vision has a compelling sense of the future. This compelling sense provides the energy needed by the organization to embark on its path to achieve its vision.

Fourth, the school leader and her team write their vision to avoid any misunderstanding. As a written document, the vision becomes a reference and rallying point for members of the organization.

A shared vision is a source of motivation to the members of the school community. Full participation in the generation of the vision is the goal of the school leader. It is through full participation that the school leader gains consensus. Full participation identifies the member's values, purpose, and desires. Ed Oakley and Doug Krug write in *Enlightened Leadership*, "Going through the process of defining a mission or vision encourages people to clarify both their organizational and individual values. The process has them clarify what is important to them and how what they want can be achieved through achieving the organization's vision."[6]

The Process of Identifying a Shared Vision

Identifying a shared vision that motivates an entire community may seem overwhelming. One way to reduce resistance and overcome anxiety in building a shared vision is to use a metaphor that symbolically represents the vision.

A *metaphor* allows us to make a comparison between two different objects. Unlike other figures of speech such as a *simile,* the metaphor does not use *like* or *as* in its expression. "At its most basic, metaphor is a rhetorical trope or a figure of speech, where a comparison is made between two seemingly unrelated objects. It is a transference of one object's characteristics to another."[7] For example, a principal says, "My assistant principal is a rock. She is a mountain." Another principal says, "My calculus teacher is fine china." Other common examples of metaphors include the Internet highway, superman or superwoman, and king of the mountain. If you listen closely, you will hear metaphors in nearly every conversation. They are common expressions.

The use of metaphors has a long and rich tradition in education. R. Elliott indicates, "Metaphors are widely used in educational discussion and fulfill a variety of functions, such as introducing fresh perspectives, making illuminating comparisons and contrasts, picking out kinds of phenomena not yet named, emphasis, illustrations, enlivening dull writing, and many others."[8] Excellent teachers use metaphors to create powerful lessons through the application of vivid imagery and to explain insights, ideas, and abstract notions. When teachers use metaphors, students connect new material to existing paradigms they hold about the world.[9] Excellent teachers use the metaphor as a natural teaching tool because the metaphor acts as a vehicle for communication.

Historically, people of all races and ages used metaphors as an integral part of their language. Owen Barfield, in his seminal work *Poetic Diction: A Study in Meaning*, says, "If we trace the meanings of a great many words—or those of the element of which they are composed—about far back as etymology can take us, we are at once made to realize that an overwhelming proportion, if not all, of them referred in earlier days to one of these two things—a solid, sensible object or some animal activity."[10]

Using metaphors is critical because "[i]n metaphor, energy is expended by the author in defamiliarizing the language and by the reader in mentally expressing the presence of a force affecting the meaning."[11] By using a sweeping, powerful metaphor, the planning team communicates with the entire school community by transcending semantic difficulties. The planning team's metaphor represents the school community's dreams and aspirations for the children who attend the school. The metaphor of the school becomes the reference point for decision making and a symbol for the school community.

A quality metaphor, grounded in each member's history and knowledge, enables school community members to express a wide array of values. Thus, the metaphor acts as an inclusive agent promoting a sense of community where people from different cultural and socioeconomic backgrounds find common ground. Using metaphors, "Possible human worlds are collaboratively constructed and transformed through the unbreakable interaction of listening and speaking. Even though conflict is pervasive, disagreement is largely relational and thus collaborative."[12]

Metaphors facilitate communication where words fail. For example, the word *watch* may refer to something you have on your wrist, a command that someone gives you, or the time a sailor spends on deck. The concept of *watch* creates different images based on our experience. Metaphors transcend this problem. Metaphors evoke a picture by taking on the characteristics of an internally held image. In this sense, metaphors take on an intangible quality.

The metaphors we use represent our internal representation of how we see the world. We then act on our internal metaphors. As we create metaphors and use them to guide our activity and actions, we establish a set of boundaries that either expand or limit our potential. In the same way that metaphors influence personal behaviors, they also affect behaviors emanating from organizations. Using metaphors to describe the image of school, gain consensus related to a mission, or to foster an inclusive community-building activity establishes our personal and organizational boundaries.

Successful leaders use constructive metaphors to expand personal and collective power. They use metaphors to communicate a vision, mission, and values. Their metaphors describe a vision that attracts others. The leader recognizes that each time he communicates with a metaphor, he is tapping into the vast reserves of experiences that exist within the leader's community. Aristotle states, "The greatest thing by far [for the leader] is to be a master of metaphor. It is the one thing that cannot be learned from others; it is also a sign of genius, since a good metaphor implies an eye for resemblance."[13]

CREATING POWERFUL METAPHOR IMAGES

Mastering the metaphor requires an ability to distinguish between *restraining* and *powerful* metaphors. Many people and organizations have restraining metaphors. Some people may call their school a dump, prison, or zoo. These metaphors restrain growth and create a negative psychological attitude toward the organization and inferentially about the speaker of the metaphor. On the other hand, if the speaker refers to the school as Camelot, Merit Scholarship factory, or home of champions, a different set of images emerges. These types of metaphors are powerful because they promote the constructive growth of those within the organization. Those associated with these metaphors are optimistic about their organizations, self, and future.

The Metaphor as the Starting Point for Constructing a Safe School Environment

The creation of an effective metaphor is a logical beginning in the creation and maintenance of an effective safe school environment because it unites the members of a school community. Each person in this process brings a personal experiential construct. These personal constructs are unique to each individual. Within this diversity, however, is a unity. Failure to seek this unity often results in organizational failure, since members, fixed on positions emanating from their personal experience, operate defensively. We eliminate this problem when we apply the metaphor construction apparatus to the creation of a shared vision. We transcend differences linked to personal experience through the creation of a metaphor representing the school community. Consider this metaphor by former United Nations ambassador Adlai Stevenson: "We travel together, passengers on a little spaceship, dependent on its vulnerable resources of air and soil; all committed for our safety to its security and peace; preserved from annihilation only by the care, the work, and I will say, the love we give our fragile craft."[14]

Metaphor as Symbol

Symbols represent an abstract or unseen construct by offering a material presence that represents the unseen. The metaphor is a symbol in the way that the Statue of Liberty symbolizes freedom to the people of the United States. Author Michael Novak tells us that symbols are specific acts or figures and are important to human beings because the symbol allows us to give significance to our beliefs, values, and activities.[15] For example, the flag is symbolic as a sign of a country, security, or a nation's values. A chain symbolizes people connecting to each other in mutual support; it can also represent community, mutual support, and strength in numbers. On the other hand, a chain can symbolize oppression, slavery, and punishment. Gibson Winter states, "Metaphors furnish clues to transformation, but they are not the powers that resist or engender such new realities. Symbols are the powers that resist change or open the way to creative change when it is needed. Root metaphors are interpretations of these founding symbols. Symbols are, in fact, metaphoric events that arise through the poetic powers of the human species."[16] The metaphor can become a symbol that represents the hopes and aspirations of the school community.

Symbols generate powerful meanings. They connect people to the past, emotional security, or an ideal. Metaphors, when used as symbols, are important to bringing about community cooperation to attain desired outcomes. Once community members accept and understand the metaphor and its symbolic representation, the metaphor communicates specific meaning. Eventually, community members need only refer to the symbol to stimulate meaning.

Metaphor as a Source of Community Building

In defining community, Martin Buber, theologian and philosopher, says, "[Community is] a living answering for one another—and mutuality, living reciprocity; not effacing the boundaries between the groups, circles, and parties, but communal recognition of the common reality and communal testing of the common responsibility."[17] Communities with a high sense of cohesion transcend their most complex problems. The metaphor contributes to building this type of community among faculty, parents, and students. It enables diverse groups to discover common ground. For example, one school community generated the metaphor of a mountain to represent their school. Parents saw the mountain symbolizing strength in the academic program and a commitment to long-held and cherished values. Teachers viewed the mountain as a symbol of struggle to gain resources to educate children. Students viewed the mountain symbolizing strength. They saw themselves climbing the mountain toward greater achievements. Metaphors such as the mountain allow groups with a wide range of experiences to experience common ownership of its symbolic interpretation. Common ownership of the metaphor's symbolic interpretation contributes to the building of community. In this process, members find no personal loss of experience, values, or identity. Community develops because the metaphor expresses communal meaning without rejecting alternative representations.

DEVELOPING A METAPHOR

The development of a metaphor is a cocreative process. It involves full participation of the team members. It is an important part of the overall strategic process. The leader makes sure that the team fully understands the concept of metaphor, by facilitating a process in which members express their ideas, attitudes, emotions, behaviors, and beliefs with metaphors.

Gene Combs and Jill Freedman offer excellent strategies for learning to think metaphorically.[18] They suggest that the team begin by talking about symbols that represent emotions or attitudes. The team can relate symbols to anger (swarm of bees), love (warm heart), laziness (sloth-like), peacefulness (clear, still lake), or another emotion or attitude. They may relate these symbols initially as similes (i.e., using *like* or *as* to express their images).

Another strategy is to tell stories. The telling of stories encourages the expression of metaphorically rich language. Team members can share positive stories of schooling they experienced when they were attending school. Team members identify the metaphors that the story-teller is using to construct meaning. In this way, the team develops greater cohesiveness through the sharing of a personal journey, the expression of attitudes and values through the application of metaphors, and the focused listening to each story. The leader encourages members to recognize the symbols represented in each story. This activity serves as a transition to the identification of symbols that represent the school.

Symbolic representation of school is a step toward creating a metaphor. In a symbolic generation activity, answers are neither right nor wrong. People discover that shared symbols stimulate a generative process during the symbolic generation activity. One principal, for example, used the metaphor of a home to symbolize the school. The principal believed that the metaphor of home generated a sense of love, warmth, caring, and security. School could become a place where the principal saw people feeling support, love, and security.

Characteristics of a Quality Metaphor

A quality metaphor has six pertinent characteristics that provide the power to communicate emotion, belief, and attitude:

1. A metaphor communicates in images.
2. A metaphor communicates through sensory experience.
3. A metaphor communicates by connecting to personal experience.
4. A metaphor communicates though the emotions it evokes.
5. A metaphor communicates through the creativity it expresses.
6. A metaphor creates meaning through its underlying values.

These six characteristics provide the structure for the metaphor to act as a catalyst encouraging the building of a sense of community. As a result, an effective metaphor serves as an anchor for commonly shared values and as the source of a school vision.

A Metaphor Communicates in Images

Our sensory experience, stored in our memory, allows us to process new data and create images. Each person interprets her sensory experience differently. Test this with your team. Show them the four images in Figure 3.1, and ask them to list what each image may represent other than its literal interpretation. Table 3.1 lists some of the possible interpretations.

These images bring up different symbolic interpretations. Each symbolic interpretation has its foundation in each person's experience. We can see, however, that a single object covers an array of interpretations. Likewise, if we reversed the process and started with words that represent values, a single image may represent each of these value words. By

Object A

Object B

Object C

Object D

Figure 3.1   Image Representations

Table 3.1. Symbolic Interpretation

Object A	Object B	Object C	Object D
Openness to others	Fairness	Archaic	Learning
Reaching out	Justice	Outdated	Knowledge
Communication	Balance	Old-fashioned	Wisdom
Receptivity	Equality	Bad-tempered	Education
Exchange of ideas	Honesty	Gruff	Information
Interaction	Integrity	Dangerous	Understanding

emphasizing image qualities, the metaphor becomes real to the user and listener. The metaphor moves from being a series of connected words to a picture in the listener's mind that takes on the aspects of momentary reality.

Another way to stimulate the use of images is to use a series of slides that show an array of pictures that encourage the creation of metaphors in each member's mind's eye. A picture of a train winding its way through the American prairie evokes a different set of metaphors. A picture of a young boy leading his younger sister across a busy street creates an image as well as a picture of a homeless person on a cold winter's day. Ask members to describe metaphors that each picture represents.

The Metaphor Communicates through Sensory Experience

Derek Bryce-Smith, professor emeritus of organic chemistry at the University of Reading in the United Kingdom, states:

> Information about the external world reaches us via the five senses—what we see, hear, etc. This information travels through the nervous system largely in the form of an electrical current of sodium ions. When this reaches the brain, it is processed by brain cells in conjunction with past information stored as memory. This interaction triggers a suitable behavioral response.[19]

The basis of all of our experience comes through our five senses: sight, hearing, taste, smell, and touch. Our senses receive information and process it by examining it against our beliefs, values, and prior experiences. Once our minds process this information, we make decisions related to what information we choose to receive and what information we choose to ignore based on our beliefs and attitudes.

Understanding how we receive and interpret data and the role that sensual stimuli play allows us to use our five senses to move the metaphor from a fictional experience to one that appears real to the mind. The greater the sensory input used in describing the metaphor, the more vivid the metaphor becomes in the listener's mind. The metaphor literally comes alive for the listener. This occurs because the sensory information allows us to anchor the metaphor to a previous experience stored in our memory. When we think of a meadow, we think of meadow in terms of our previous experience. My description of a meadow—a place that has a clear, ice-cold brook gurgling through the middle of waist-high golden grass that sways to a gentle summer's breeze, while overhead, a hawk glides gracefully through the sky, occasionally sending out a shrieking call to its mate—comes from my experience. The meadow that I remember is easy to recall because I link each of my five senses to this memory. The application of the five senses to the metaphor helps to anchor the metaphor to personal experience and enhances recall.

The Metaphor Communicates by Connecting to Personal Experience

Connecting to experience is critical to creating a powerful metaphor. Each person's experience is his history. This history is a set of images attached to emotion or attitudes. This history allows us to evaluate the present situation against our experience. For example, I could use the metaphor of a clear, peaceful lake to represent the harmony that exists among faculty, but some faculty may not have the same experience I do. A faculty member may have a negative experience of a lake. His experience, being different, elicits a different response. To identify an inclusive metaphor, the team needs to construct a metaphor embracing the positive emotions, attitudes, and beliefs of *all* members. This is a time-consuming process. It is more like the planting and nurturing of a seed than the picking of a fruit. This process requires the validation of each member's collective and shared experiences.

The Metaphor Communicates through the Emotions It Evokes

Metaphors evoke strong, positive, and constructive emotions. A metaphor evokes different emotions for each person. Positive emotions communicate the school's mission to a diverse community. It is the emotion that team members connect to the metaphor that serves as a source of energy for the school community by acting as a catalyst or motivator. "Remember the Alamo" is a metaphor that provokes strong emotions in many Texans. On the other hand, negative emotions such as anger, hate, envy, fear, anxiety, and hopelessness can disempower an organization. A metaphor by its application evokes positive or negative emotions. Consider the metaphor "The weight of the world is on my shoulders." In one scene, create an image of a person standing with the planet Earth on his shoulders. In another scene, create an image of the same person standing on top of the world exulting in his success. The metaphor symbolizes something different in each scene.

The Metaphor Communicates through the Creativity It Expresses

Creativity is our ability to take what we know and rearrange that knowledge to serve new functions. "Gutenberg took the wine press and the die/punch and produced a printing press. Thus, a simple definition of creativity is the action of combining previously uncombined elements. Creativity is the ability to generate novel and useful ideas and solutions to everyday problems and challenges."[20] Constructing a metaphor is a creative process, and the resulting metaphor should be a creative expression.

Techniques can help produce a creative metaphor. One technique is a *forced analogy*. In a forced analogy, the object is to have team members compare the concept of school with another idea or object that has nothing in common with the school. When you force the analogy, you gain fresh perceptions regarding the notion of schooling. One way to force these relationships is to have a set of pictures that generate ideas. For example, pictures can include the United Nations building, a football team, or the Grand Canyon.[21]

As each member participates in the forced analogy, this cocreative process contributes to the development of a new generation of metaphors. Often, this process results in a synergy that produces unexpected results. One group, for example, at Brewer Elementary School in San Antonio, Texas, developed the metaphor of a spaceship hurtling through space exploring vast unknown areas. As the spaceship sped through space, those aboard adapted to changing situations and invented creative solutions to new problems.

The Metaphor Creates Meaning through Its Underlying Value

Our values are inherent in our actions and expressed in our metaphors. A person talking about home mentions values such as love, security, and acceptance. A principal, who speaks of the team, speaks of values such as sharing, collaboration, and fairness. Similarly, the colors our metaphors express also demonstrate value. We speak of lively colors, warm colors, cold and stale colors, or depressing colors. Color is a way of outwardly expressing an inward reality. Metaphors inherently express values since they portray a picture seen in the speaker's mind. As the speaker describes her metaphor, she embeds values within her picture.

These essential characteristics of a quality metaphor provide four important outcomes:

1. The metaphor becomes an anchoring reference for future strategic discussions.
2. The metaphor becomes a source of motivation to increase role competence.
3. The metaphor serves as the basis for developing a greater sense of community.
4. The metaphor links goals and mission to a collaboratively developed vision.

IDENTIFYING A METAPHOR TO SYMBOLIZE THE SCHOOL

The team's responsibility is to create a metaphor symbolizing their school. This process allows team members to discover common ground and build a spirit of community. The leader facilitates this process by identifying personal metaphors that motivated them in the past. For example, John, a middle school teacher, reported that his father was in the hospital. His father's condition was terminal. John had to exert leadership—he knew he had to be an anchor for his family. John would be strong and hold his extended family together. He pictured himself as a source of security and stability. His anchor metaphor strengthened him throughout this challenge. Team members, like John in this example, develop a personal metaphor before working on a school metaphor. When each member conceptualizes her metaphor with its inherent values, she describes the metaphor to the group. Members should explain the metaphor's meaning by describing what it symbolizes. For example, Mary Garza, a sixth grade teacher, described a river that expressed the values of constant movement, power, flow, and connection. Mary felt the metaphor symbolized potential, resources, and life-supporting energy.

The principal, as the group leader, actively assists members in illustrating their metaphor. As members express their metaphor, the principal makes sure that members apply the list of quality metaphor characteristics to their metaphor (see Table 3.2).

Table 3.2 Matching the Metaphor to Quality Characteristics

Quality Characteristic	Application to the Metaphor
The metaphor communicates in images.	Applies/Does not apply
The metaphor communicates through sensory experience.	Applies/Does not apply
The metaphor communicates by connecting to personal experience.	Applies/Does not apply
The metaphor communicates though the emotions it evokes.	Applies/Does not apply
The metaphor communicates through the creativity it expresses.	Applies/Does not apply
The metaphor creates meaning through its underlying values.	Applies/Does not apply

DESCRIBING THE METAPHOR'S MEANING

The metaphor communicates values, mission, and vision directly to the community. It serves to unite diverse community groups and transcend cultural, racial, and ethnic differences. Each member's metaphor communicates a potential way to transcend these differences. For example, some members may share a metaphor emphasizing cooperation. Others metaphors may emphasize achievement or respect. Teachers may use metaphors of gardeners, spaceship pilots, or an atom to express values related to the educational process. Whatever the result, each person's metaphor creates a climate of generative creativity and stimulates a process that empowers people to think about metaphors that are inclusive and large enough to embrace all values vital to members of the school community.

The message of the metaphor is in its underlying value structure. For example, the metaphor of a greenhouse projects the value of life. The metaphor of an atom projects the value of power. The metaphor of a mountain projects the value of strength. The metaphor of home projects the value of love and security. The metaphor of church projects the value of belonging and peace. The following table identifies values associated with each of the groups in the school community.

Table 3.3 Identifying Associated Values with Different Groups

Students	Parents	Teachers	Community
Inclusion	Safety	Learning	Contribution
Success	Hope	Personal fulfillment	Value
Desire	Respect	Commitment	Integrity
Friendship	Collaboration	Cooperation	Responsibility
Safety	Guidance	Respect	Duty
Acceptance	Value	Safety	Loyalty

The school leader uses this process to move the team toward consensus on shared values (see chapter 2). As members express the values inherent in their metaphor, the school leader lists the values on newsprint (see Table 3.4). Finding ways to cluster values simplifies discussion. For example, team members may cluster love and caring with compassion.

Table 3.4 Sample Chart of Values Associated with Significant Groups

Parents	Students	Teachers	Community Members	Administrators
Safety	Caring	Learning	Efficiency	Responsibility
Responsibility	Safety	Respect	Effectiveness	Duty
Caring	Friendliness	Responsibility	Loyalty	Civility
Nurturing	Forgiveness	Cooperation	Respect	Safety
Fairness	Responsibility	Caring	Responsibility	Collaboration

DEVELOPING A COMMON METAPHOR

From the common value list, the team develops a metaphor that inclusively embraces and expresses all represented values. The metaphor transcends time limitations and represents the past, present, and future. This metaphor is inclusive and has symbolism for members of the team, school, and community. Team members work at this process until they agree on a metaphor that represents their values. The school leader and team commit the metaphor to writing to avert disagreement related to meaning.

When the team reaches consensus on their metaphor, its values, and symbolism, the team is ready to share the metaphor with the school community. Team members explain how the metaphor empowers teachers, parents, students, community members, and administrators. They explain how the metaphor empowers the school community to reach safe school goals. They explain how the metaphor applies to the school environment. They explain how the metaphor applies to relationships with the community, parents, teachers, the school board, and administrators. This process of communication is subtle when team members use the metaphor in professional conversations regarding the school and its programs. The metaphor becomes the symbol for a safe school environment.

EXAMPLE OF A DYNAMIC METAPHOR

The Riverside High School team developed the metaphor of a greenhouse.

We build the greenhouse with glass so all people can look into it. The glass walls communicate an invitation to those outside the greenhouse to enter. The greenhouse is open and fully accessible. Anyone can enter, wander around, and gain a sense of peace, serenity, and strength from observing what is occurring in the greenhouse. Those who choose to enter the greenhouse experience a sense of life. They see all types of plants at different stages of growth and life. Each plant is healthy. A gardener personally takes care of each plant. On closer observation, one notices many plants. Some plants are tall and have many leaves; other plants are short and have many flowers. Other plants are in dormancy.

Within the greenhouse, one sees a variety of environments that positively affect the plants. One part of the greenhouse is moist, while another part is dry and desertlike. The gardener knows the environment that the plants need and uses that knowledge to construct an atmosphere critical to the growth of the plants. If you stayed long enough in the greenhouse, you would notice that the gardener uses the right amount of sunlight supplemented with artificial light at night. The gardener applies the same process to the nutrients that each plant needs. The gardener knows that too much of one nutrient at any given time would be harmful to the plants. The gardener's knowledge and experience determine the application of the nutrients.

Each plant in the greenhouse expresses its individuality. Size does not determine the beauty of the plant; the beauty expresses itself at the various stages it passes through as it grows into its full potential. A small plant is as beautiful as a large plant. A cactus in bloom is as beautiful as a tomato plant with red and green tomatoes or an orange tree. A palm tree's beauty is as unique as that of a rosemary plant.

The gardener represents those in the school community who have responsibility for educating children. The plants symbolize students, teachers, staff, and administrators. The gardener's job is to serve the needs of the plants, to give the plants an environment that is safe and conducive to their growth. The gardener knows each plant in the same way that an excellent teacher knows each student or how an administrator knows each teacher's strengths and weaknesses. The gardener is not afraid to prune a plant. However, the gardener never injures a plant. The difference between pruning and injuring is significant to the gardener. Whatever action the gardener applies to a plant is always meant for that plant's future and positive development and its contribution to the overall beauty of the greenhouse.

Analysis of the Riverside High School Metaphor: The Greenhouse

The Riverside High School metaphor of the greenhouse has the six essential characteristics for a quality metaphor. The following analysis of this school's metaphor demonstrates its potent effect within the community. Use this analysis to guide your team in analyzing their own metaphor.

The Metaphor Communicates in Images

Each of us has seen a greenhouse. Those living in northern climates see the importance of the greenhouse in winter when life outside the greenhouse is dormant. On the other hand, those in warmer climates recognize that the greenhouse symbolizes the constant evolution of new growth. The Riverside team described the exterior and interior of the greenhouse. The description of plants was clear. The role of the gardener represents teachers who work with students, colleagues, parents, and administrators. This pattern is true for administrators and parents. A thriving greenhouse ignores no plants.

The Metaphor Communicates through Sensory Experience

The metaphor of the greenhouse is a panoply of rich colors. The colors in the greenhouse represent life and the values associated with life. The metaphor speaks about the dark greens of each plant or the light-colored green on the plants. It speaks of colorful flowers in bloom and of oranges and red and green tomatoes.

The Metaphor Communicates by Connecting to Personal Experience

The Riverside school community communicates the metaphor through personal growth experiences. The metaphor of different plants at different stages of development coexists with the Swiss psychologist Jean Piaget's stages of human development. The greenhouse symbolizes the individual nature of the learning cycle. It also symbolizes pruning. The gardener looks at each plant in the same way that the teacher looks at each student recognizing individual differences. This is a powerful metaphor for parents who recognize that the school sees their children as unique.

The Metaphor Communicates through the Emotions It Evokes

The metaphor of greenhouse stresses the emotion of hope. The people of Riverside High School feel there is an emotional serenity in a greenhouse. Teachers in this group saw their metaphor of a greenhouse representing a place of learning and serenity where classrooms, although filled with vibrancy, are peaceful. The greenhouse metaphor invokes emotions of growth and caring. It evokes the emotion associated with acceptance. They saw the greenhouse as the home of many different species that live and grow with each other. These emotions refer to how members of the school community relate to each other and to the greater community.

The Metaphor Communicates through the Creativity It Expresses

As the group spoke about the metaphor of a greenhouse, they discussed what was inside the greenhouse. Their description of the greenhouse became deeper and richer through continued conversations. The team spoke of different types of soils and plants. They described each plant in full detail. They described what it was like to be a small plant among many tall plants. Members reflected on how empowering it felt when each plant received personal attention. The team went into detail in describing the gardener's qualities. They saw these qualities applying to teachers, students, parents, and administrators.

The Metaphor Creates Meaning through Its Underlying Values

The Riverside High School team expressed values in colors they discovered in the greenhouse. They visualized the greenhouse filled with soft green symbolizing life and growth. They used red to express energy and vibrancy. They used yellow, red, and purple to symbolize peace and serenity. The gardener expressed the values of attention, caring, and compassion. The greenhouse expressed the values of warmth, life, inclusion, and acceptance. The team, by embracing the metaphor of the greenhouse, created an inclusive symbol that had the power to contain the values critical to the members of the community.

SUMMARY

Creating an inclusive vision is essential to uniting members of the school community in a common cause. Without a common vision, there is no unifying theme to motivate members to journey toward uncharted waters. The creation of a metaphor transcends many of the linguistic problems that result from different meanings applied to words. A metaphor is a means for groups to express deeply held values in pictures that we commonly understand. It allows each person to interpret its meaning in light of personal knowledge and experience. A positive metaphor is requisite for constructing a safe school environment.

The metaphor becomes a focal point to identify values, develop strategies, and build a sense of community. It gains viability with application. In using a metaphor to create a vision for the school, team members move beyond cultural and individual differences. The metaphor weaves multiple values into a single vision. The vision that emanates from the metaphor is unique to each school, representing not only the school but its cultural context and members of school community as well.

The vision-metaphor empowers the school community. The vision-metaphor generates a synergistic element that enables people to relate to the school at an emotional level based on their history. Connecting people at this level creates links among constituents and between each constituent and the organization. These linkages become the core of conversation and a stimulus for organizational learning. A quality metaphor has six defining characteristics. When we apply all six characteristics to the metaphor selected for the school, the metaphor has the potential to serve as a central convening point for dialogue. A constructive, inspiring vision is the starting point for an effective strategic safe school proposal.

Putting It Together: Advancing with Vigilance	✓
Does everyone understand the adopted metaphor? Does everyone agree that the metaphor represents the vision for the school organization? Do the identified values fit the metaphor? Do all the characteristics of a quality metaphor apply to the metaphor? Is the metaphor a core component of educational conversations within the school community? Does the metaphor provide the sense of a shared vision?	

NOTES

1. "Components of a Vision," North Central Regional Educational Laboratory, <http://www.ncrel.org/sdrs/areas/issues/educatrs/leadrshp/le1comps.htm> (4 April 2000).

2. Thomas J. Sergiovanni, *The Principalship: A Reflective Practice Perspective*, 3d ed. (Boston: Allyn & Bacon, 1995), 132.

3. A. Lorri Manasse, "Vision and Leadership: Paying Attention to Intention," *Peabody Journal of Education* 63, no. 1 (1986): 150–73.

4. Raymond Calabrese, Gary Short, and Sally Zepeda, *Hands-on Leadership Means for Principals* (Larchmont, N.Y.: Eye on Education, 1965), 66.

5. Thomas Peters, *Thriving on Chaos: Handbook for a Management Revolution* (New York: Harper & Row, 1987), 486.

6. Ed Oakley and Doug Krug, *Enlightened Leadership* (New York: Simon & Schuster, 1993), 173.

7. Ronnie Manalo Ruiz, "Metaphor," Georgia Institute of Technology, <http://www.lcc.gatech.edu/gallery/rhetoric/terms/metaphor.html> (10 April 2000).

8. R. Elliott, "Metaphor, Imagination and Conceptions of Education," in *Metaphors of Education*, ed. William Taylor (London: Heinemann Educational Books, 1984), 39.

9. Living Lab Curriculum, "The Magic of Metaphor," A Living Laboratory: Volcanoes, <http://volcano.und.nodak.edu/vwdocs/msh/llc/is/mom.html> (3 April 2000).

10. Owen Barfield, *Poetic Diction: A Study in Meaning* (Middletown, Conn.: Wesleyan University Press, 1973), 63.

11. William Covino and David Jolliffe, *Rhetoric: Concepts, Definitions, Boundaries* (Boston: Allyn & Bacon, 1995), 106.

12. Gemma Fiumara, *The Metaphoric Process: Connections between Language and Life* (New York: Rutledge, 1995), 9.

13. Aristotle, "De Poetica," prepared by Brad Shepherd, Georgia Institute of Technology (12 March 1996), <http://www.lcc.gatech.edu/gallery/rhetoric/noframes/figures/aristotle.html> (5 April 2000).

14. Adlai Stevenson, quoted in Richard Armstrong and Edward Wakin, *You Can Still Change the World* (New York: Harper & Row, 1978), 73.

15. Michael Novak, *The Experience of Nothingness* (New York: Harper & Row, 1970).

16. Gibson Winter, cited in "Significance: Metaphor, Analogy, Symbol and Pattern," Governance through Metaphor Project, <http://www.uia.org/metaphor/13sigana.htm> (3 April 2000).

17. Martin Buber, *Pointing the Way* (Freeport, N.Y.: Books for Libraries Press, 1957), 102.

18. Gene Combs and Jill Freedman, *Symbol, Story, and Ceremony: Using Metaphor in Individual Family Therapy* (New York: Norton, 1990).

19. D. Bryce-Smith, "Crime and Nourishment," CMHC Systems, Mental Health Net <http://www.cmhc.com/perspectives/articles/art03964.htm> (5 April 2000).

20. "Definitions of Creativity," Creativity Web Home Page (1999) <http://www.ozemail.com.au/~caveman/Creative/Basics/definitions.htm> (10 April 2000).

21. Robert Olson, "The Art of Creative Thinking," information taken from <http://www.ozemail.com.au/~caveman/Creative/Techniques/forced_analogy.htm> (5 April 2000)

CHAPTER FOUR

Shaping the Organizational Belief System

This chapter shows how to influence the attitudes of school community members so that each member embraces an attitude of high expectations regarding the development and maintenance of a safe school environment. The effective school leader knows that developing a successful safe school is a complex process driven by an optimistic belief system. A positive organizational and personal belief system is at the core of all successful organizations and people. This chapter shows the school leader how to harness the power of a personal and collective belief system to shape expectations.

In this chapter, you will

- define empowering and limiting beliefs,
- understand the application of the belief system to effective school safe school practices, and
- use the belief system to build confidence among school community members in developing an effective strategy.

THE POWER OF THE BELIEF SYSTEM

All of our attitudes have cognitive, behavioral, and emotional ingredients. Central to reshaping our attitudes is our belief system. In this chapter, the *belief system* refers to that part of our mind that interprets messages, either external or internal, and perceives them as real. A belief is the mental acceptance and conviction that something is true, exists, or is correct. Once we accept an idea as true or valid (a belief), it shapes our actions. Consequently, our beliefs define many of our outcomes. In a personal sense, our beliefs affect our health. "Surprisingly, just believing that you have control—even when you really don't—can affect your physiological response to stress, and your health. Because optimists are more active than pessimists, they are more likely to do something for the health."[1] In an organizational sense, personal beliefs held by members affect the organization's behavior and outcomes. "The values and beliefs of individuals affect their behavior and in leaders they influence the vision leaders hold of their school or district."[2]

We are not born with beliefs. We acquire beliefs as we grow. Every belief that you have at this moment you received from an external source. You acquired these beliefs from your family, social organizations such as churches and schools, and others beliefs that you freely chose after weighing available evidence. In general, our beliefs help us to put meaning on what we perceive to be happening in our lives. The motivational speaker Anthony Robbins states, "Beliefs are generalizations about our past, based on our interpretations of painful and pleasurable experiences. Most of us do not consciously decide what we're going to believe and we treat our beliefs as if they're realities."[3]

What we believe becomes real whether or not it exists. Because our perceptions are real to us, we act as if the perception were real, even if it is not. For example, imagine yourself walking down a deserted city street during the night hours. You hear a noise coming from an alley. Your mind starts racing and imagining that a mugger lurks in the alley waiting to attack you. Your heart beats faster; your mind races for solutions to this problem. Suddenly, two stray dogs emerge from the alley. You rub your hand against your head, your heart stops racing, and your mind quiets down. The noise in the alley caused your mind to jump to an erroneous conclusion, and your body responded to that conclusion as if it were real. In effect, we express beliefs as expectations and act out these beliefs in our attitudes and actions. In an educational sense, teachers frequently see students with a poor self-image act as if it were their actual image. They see capable students with a low level of personal expectations fail. They see students with limited ability, yet with high expectations, succeed. These teachers witness the power of the belief system in each of these students.

Our beliefs are complex and take the shape of a belief system. Neurolinguistic psychologists Robert Dilts, Tim Hallbom, and Suzi Smith say, "Belief systems are the large frame around any change work. However, if people really believe they cannot do something, they are going to find an unconscious way to keep the change from occurring. They'll find a way to interrupt the results to conform with their existing beliefs."[4] This is true in many dysfunctional or low-performing schools. Prevailing beliefs in these types of schools include the belief that change is impossible, teachers and administrators are adversaries, teachers and administrators view the community and parents as adversaries, there is one best way to teach and discipline children, and authoritarian and hierarchical paradigms are the most effective ways of organizing schools.[5]

Our belief system determines how we act, feel, and relate to our environment. We base our decisions on what we believe to be real in our environment. Our belief system filters information through our five senses. It then projects a picture of reality based on how it organizes and analyzes the sensory data. This picture may range from accurate to inaccurate. Our belief system, since it is so susceptible to manipulation, allows us to make an idea, concept, or image real. Researchers view our belief system as one of our most powerful change tools. We can use our belief system to our advantage or disadvantage.

EXAMINING THE MEDICAL MODEL OF THE BELIEF SYSTEM

Medical researchers discovered a synergy between the doctor and patient. When they activate the belief-oriented synergy, patients heal more quickly and live longer. The belief system between doctor and patient has a clearly identifiable pattern with three major components: patient, doctor, and treatment. The patient believes that the doctor facilitates healing. The doctor believes that the patient is a partner in the healing process. Together, the doctor and patient believe that the prescribed treatment heals the patient. Herbert Benson, Harvard University medical researcher, writes, "Our brains are wired for beliefs and expectancies. When activated, the body can respond as it would if the belief were a reality, producing deafness or thirst, health or illness."[6]

Defining Beliefs

Our beliefs define us. They are personal and collective. They are personal in the sense we are unique. Our beliefs are also collective and operate in social environments. Our workplace is a social organization where people with individual beliefs come together and operate with a common set of beliefs. Beliefs are limiting when they prevent a person from achieving full potential. One person's belief is a journey with little hope. Another person's belief is a journey filled with hope and opportunity. Beliefs, whether they are empowering or limiting, affect each person.

In my Change Class, I asked each student to predict the age at which he or she believes he or she will die. The vast majority of my students give themselves a limited time span. None believe they will live to be ninety years old. One person believed that he would die in his fifties because his father and grandfather had died in their fifties. It was evident from the student's physical appearance that he was on a path of a self-fulfilling prophecy. Events in his family taught this student "Men in this family die young."

How the Belief System Works

The belief system filters sensory data received through our five senses. As we process this data, our beliefs determine whether the data are true or false. It does not matter, however, if the data are true or false. We readily confirm data that bolster our beliefs and block data that challenge our beliefs.

Each time we reinforce our beliefs, they become more deeply rooted in our subconscious. When we challenge these beliefs, we immediately defend them. For example, a Latino woman related that people convinced her that she could not succeed in college. Consequently, she quit school and became a maid. Years later, someone recognized her potential and encouraged her to return to school. Today she is an outstanding teacher. In effect, our beliefs

- express a certainty about people, things, ideas, or experiences;
- define our environment;
- give us a sense of control over our circumstances; and
- provide a roadmap to make life predictable and meaningful.

Belief and Performance

We can relate our beliefs to our level of performance. To perform successfully, we must have a personal belief in our ability to transform our environment. This personal belief allows us to transcend the possibility of failure and initiate positive action. Oftentimes, skilled teachers and administrators fail to transform their school environment because limiting beliefs drive their actions. Ironically, these limiting beliefs are difficult to replace with positive beliefs. Researchers call this belief *perseverance*.

According to psychologists Sharon Brehm and Saul Kassin, *belief perseverance* is "[t]he tendency to stick to initial beliefs even after they have been discredited. It is easier to get people to build a theory than to convince them to tear it down."[7] *Limiting beliefs* are self-imposed restrictions we place on organizations or ourselves. *Empowering beliefs,* on the other hand, eliminate restrictions and place no cap on potential achievement. When the school leader assists teachers, students, and parents in discarding limiting beliefs, he increases their level of performance.

A person's and organization's performance improves as they replace limiting beliefs with empowering beliefs. For example, sport teams operate with individual and collective beliefs. A professional basketball player believes he has the ability to make the all-star team. At the same time, he has a belief that his team can win the championship. This person has a separate set of beliefs from every other member of his team. His beliefs are unique. He brings his beliefs to his team because he operates in a social and collective environment. His beliefs influence the team as well as himself.

CREATING A POWER-FILLED BELIEF SYSTEM

The school leader can create an empowering belief system for her school. Effective school leaders anchor an empowering belief system in communal activity. One powerful communal activity the school leader can use with her team is the use of shared stories. *Story sharing* is a powerful tool. "People need to talk, to tell about what has happened to them, and they need to hear about what has happened to others, especially when the others are people they care about or who might have had experiences relevant to the hearer's own life."[8] Through the sharing of stories, individual members discover that their team consists of skilled, competent people. For example, Jason Scotman, an assistant principal, shared his story of school officials labeling him as emotionally disturbed as a grade school child. His parents did not believe the diagnosis. The label never left Jason until he graduated from high school. He went to college and graduated with honors, determined to enter teaching. Jason's success story demonstrated to others that Jason has a history of successful performance. It also renewed Jason's sense of self-confidence.

When team members share performance success stories, the sense of organizational confidence grows. *Confidence* is the feeling of self-assurance or group assurance. Skilled performance and confidence are directly proportional. They are synergistic. Without confidence, there is no skilled performance; without skilled performance, there is only the illusion of confidence. Building confidence and increasing skilled performance materialize out of a refined, optimistic belief system. Understanding the three parts to the belief system is fundamental to this process.

The Three Parts to the Belief System

The belief system of human beings and within organizational culture has three equally important parts:

- The school leader
- Team members and the people they represent
- The prescription

The leader brings a set of skills and abilities to this process. Leadership

> provides an environment that promotes individual contributions to the organization's work. Leaders develop and maintain collaborative relationships formed during the development and adoption of the shared vision. They form teams, support team efforts, develop the skills groups and individuals need, and provide the necessary resources, both human and material, to fulfill the shared vision.[9]

To be effective, the leader has a clear understanding of the school and community's expectations. The following equation expresses leadership:

$$\text{Leadership} = (\text{Ecological needs} + \text{Perceived needs} + \text{Source of the problem})/\text{Time}$$

Ecological needs refer to the school organization's needs, expressed or unexpressed, that are physically present and identifiable within the school. These needs include the physical condition of the building, the decision making structure, and the layout of the building as well as its size. The school, for example, is overcrowded and using portables to compensate for the overcrowding.

Perceived needs reflect the community members' attitudes and ideas as to how to make the school more effective. These needs are more instinctual than reasoned. They are more linked to beliefs than reflected in data.

For example, the reorganization of a large high school in San Antonio, Texas, conflicted with the belief of community members who did not see the size of the school as a problem. The superintendent received significant public criticism for supporting reorganization.

The source of the problem is different from the apparent symptoms. When school leaders focus their attention solely on symptoms, any relief is temporary. It is important that school leaders address the source of the problem for permanent relief.

Time is not static; rather, it is both linear and ambiguous. It is linear in that there are sixty minutes in an hour, twenty-four hours in a day, and seven days in a week. It is ambiguous because time has different meanings to different people. For some, time stands still. For others, there is not enough time. Time is critical to the leader because it establishes the boundaries for action. Time runs out for the school leader who neglects to develop a comprehensive safe school plan. The effective school leader focuses simultaneously on ecology, perception, and source. This school leader is also aware of time constraints and factors time into the group's safe school planning process.

In a medical sense, the prescription is the treatment that the physician asks the patient to apply to his ailment. The concept of prescription is directly applicable to the process of creating a safe school. Whatever problems exist within any organization, there needs to be an effective prescription that leaders and members believe leads to the resolution of the problem.

A primary factor in considering the application of a prescription is that all parties must believe in the prescription's efficacy. The belief in the prescription is crucial. Researchers consistently report that placebos given to patients have the same or even greater affect than the actual medicine. Dilts and his coauthors report that researchers studying more than one hundred cancer patients who were diagnosed as terminally ill and who have survived for more than ten years found only one common theme among all of these surviving cancer patients. The common theme among cancer patients who had survived more than ten years was that they believed that their treatment and physician were critical components in their healing. They had a deep belief that the treatment that they followed was directly responsible for their survival.[10] The positive and optimistic believe of the school leader and team members in the prescription they develop to create a safe school will influence the prescription's outcome.

DEVELOPING SKILLED PERFORMANCE

Understanding the three parts to the belief system allows the school leader to generate a sense of confidence and increased skilled performance among team members. Team members increase their skilled performance when they recognize that they are important components to the development of a safe school environment. The school leader facilitates this growth by team members by asking them to reflect on the following questions:

- Do I have something important to contribute to the development of a safe school?
- Do I feel that this task is important?
- Do I desire to be part of this process?
- Have my background and training led me to believe that this is where I belong?

These questions allow members to express personal confidence in their work because each person is more aware of the widespread confidence within the team. Consequently, confidence contagiously spreads throughout the team. The team's increased confidence permits skill level assessment in five domains:

1. Social skills
2. Decision making
3. Problem solving
4. Judgment
5. Follow-through

Assessing each of these domains allows team members to identify personal and group strengths and weaknesses. The identification of a collective set of strengths develops a sense of confidence in the group's potential skilled performance (see Tables 4.1 through Table 4.5).

The leader uses the results of this activity to emphasize the team's history of skilled performance. It also identifies areas where the team needs to increase levels of skilled performance. Recognizing this need, the team actively recruits skilled performers from the school community to be part of the team. Applying a baseball analogy, the manager of a team would not seek an additional pitcher if the manager felt the team's weakness was in catching. The manager seeks to find a competent catcher to eliminate this weakness from his team. Using this approach, the leader facilitates the team's skilled performance and increases team confidence.

CONFIDENCE

Confidence is the state of self-assurance that leaves little doubt that an action will succeed. According to Charles Garfield, author of *Peak*

Table 4.1 Domain 1: Social Skills—Identification of Team Members with High Degrees of Social Skills

	Current Skill Strength	Not an Area of Strength
Has a high degree of comfort in interacting with people of diverse backgrounds		
Communicates with people of diverse backgrounds		
Is able and willing to listen to people from diverse backgrounds		
Can involve people from diverse backgrounds		

Table 4.2 Domain 2: Decision Making—Identification of Team Members with High Degrees of Decision-Making Skills

	Current Skill Strength	Not an Area of Strength
Can make decisions under stress		
Makes collaborative decisions		
Generates alternatives before making a decision		
Collects information before making a decision		

Table 4.3 Domain 3: Problem Solving—The Ability to Identify Both the Cause and the Source of Problems

	Current Skill Strength	Not an Area of Strength
Can identify the problem		
Is able to locate and identify the source of a problem		
Distinguishes causes from symptoms		
Aims to solve problems collaboratively		

Table 4.4 Domain 4: Judgment—Identification of Team Members with the Ability to Make Sound Judgments

	Current Skill Strength	Not an Area of Strength
Demonstrates ability to make sound judgments		
Makes accurate judgments of situations		
Has wisdom to know when to change directions		
Has integrity-driven judgment		

Table 4.5 Domain 5: Follow-Through—Identification of Team Members with the Ability to Follow-Through

	Current Skill Strength	Not an Area of Strength
Demonstrates ability to follow through on commitments		
Manages time so that responsibilities are completed		
Is able to complete task with little or no supervision		
Perceives what is required and then acts decisively		

Performance, "Confidence reflects the belief that we are not bound by past records, genetics, or conditioning, but that we can operate as free beings, capable of influencing to a significant extent the course of our lives."[11] Confidence occurs in personal and communal contexts. People have confidence in leaders because they can reference the leader's history of success. Industrial psychologists tell us that past performance is a predictor of future performance. Those people who have a high record of accomplishment of success have a history of success. However, it is not a perfect history of success; it is a history that has occasional failure. People who know only successes can seldom overcome failure. Our personal history does not have to be 100 percent successes. Our personal history needs to identify a clear pattern of success.

The leader increases the confidence among team members by transforming personal confidence into group confidence. One can be confident in personal skills and succeed at a solo activity such as skiing. However, creating an effective safe school strategy is not a solo activity. To be successful, each team member needs to rely on all members of the group. They need to receive constant feedback. As the team develops an effective safe school plan, the team's confidence increases. The team members' response to the team's progress determines their level of confidence in their abilities, ideas, and experience. In effect, the leader guides the team in gaining confidence by being a source of inspiration and leadership. Conversely, team members are the source of motivation and inspiration to the leader. It is a synergistic activity in which both, leader and follower, need each other.

The following three-part confidence check, taken by the school leader and group members individually, determines team confidence levels. There are no right or wrong answers. The three-part confidence check, however, needs to be a source of discussion that leads to greater team honesty, trust, and confidence.

Part 1: Confidence in Team Leadership

1. The leader works effectively with team members.
   Yes   Maybe   No
2. Team members can recall successes under the leader's direction.
   Yes   Maybe   No
3. Team members respect the leader.
   Yes   Maybe   No
4. Team members seek to participate with the leader on challenging projects.
   Yes   Maybe   No

Answers to these questions provide an estimated level of confidence that team members have in the leader. The school leader can build the team's confidence by seeking small and public successes. As confidence grows in the school leader's commitment, ability to lead, and vision, the team's commitment to the leader increases.

Part 2: Communication and Acceptance of the School Leader's Vision

1. The leader has a clear vision of effective safe school practices.
   Yes   Maybe   No
2. The leader communicates a clear vision of a safe school environment.
   Yes   Maybe   No
3. Team members embrace the school leader's vision of a safe school environment.
   Yes   Maybe   No
4. Team members feel guided by the school leader's vision of a safe school environment.
   Yes   Maybe   No

The leader has to have a clear vision of safe school practices to inspire confidence. Warren Bennis says that a vision is "capacity to create and communicate a compelling vision of a desired state of affairs."[12] Allow your vision to develop—it takes time. You need to be reflective. It is a thinking process.

Part 3: Acting with and Communicating Confidence
1. Does the team communicate confidence that they can provide a safe and secure environment?
              Yes   Maybe   No
2. Do the team's vocabulary, agenda, actions, and attitudes communicate confidence?
              Yes   Maybe   No
3. Is the school community aware of the team's successes?
              Yes   Maybe   No
4. Is the team acting with certainty?
              Yes   Maybe   No

The school leader and team have to exude confidence in their task. The members of the school community will see any slight hesitation as anxiety and a lack of confidence. Confidence projected by the team onto the school community prepares the ground for the implementation of the safe school plan.

DEVELOPING WIDESPREAD CONFIDENCE IN THE TEAM'S IDEAS

We develop widespread confidence in our ideas by testing them. The school leader and her team constantly scrutinize and test new ideas and evaluate how members of the school community respond to these ideas. This process is a way for the school leader to expand the involvement of other people. The school leader connects new ideas to the member's experiential base and learns from the feedback provided by the member to the new idea. President John F. Kennedy, when debating whether the United States should support the Bay of Pigs Invasion, surrounded himself with intelligent people who felt that they had to provide the president with reinforcing information. President Kennedy received positive feedback regarding the proposition to support Cuban exiles in their invasion of Cuba. His advisers failed to provide him with critical and honest feedback. Providing critical feedback, criticizing his ideas, and putting his ideas to a test of intellectual scrutiny were lacking; therefore, the Bay of Pigs Invasion was a failure.

The school leader also generates confidence when proposals are consistent with effective practice. The effective school leader knows the difference between effective and questionable practice. Effective practice is consistent with the values within the community. Ann Lockwood writes in *Leaders for Tomorrow's Schools,* "[Effective school practice] places a premium on reform that comes from the grassroots and maintains a respectful attitude toward the local context and community. Central to the Coalition's [Coalition for Essential Schools, or CES] philosophy is the belief that no two good schools are alike."[13]

Effective practice in one community is not necessarily effective practice in another community. Effective practice depends on the context and the community. For example, sex education taught in public schools in a community with a conservative religious base would raise political opposition, whereas the same program in a liberal community receives formidable support.

DEVELOPING PERSONAL CONFIDENCE

Increasing confidence is a planned process requiring a systematic approach. Initially, the school leader and his team reach out to the school community for involvement. Teachers, students, and parents make suggestions regarding the design of a safe school environment. Each group has a specific perspective. Members' perceptions are personal; they are neither right nor wrong. Identifying perceptions allows the school leader to understand each member's starting point in developing an effective safe school environment.

After collecting suggestions from school community members, the team evaluates each suggestion in terms of its viability and contribution to creating a safe school environment. The school leader and team can use Table 4.6 as a guideline for rating each suggestion's potential effectiveness.

The team identifies the efficacy of these ideas in the school's cultural and socioeconomic context. This process has three parts.

First, community members identify their level of expectations regarding a safe school environment. This step is important since any strategy,

Table 4.6 Rating Potential Effectiveness of Suggestions

		Identified Suggestion and Rated Effectiveness			
Identified Suggestion	*Effective*	*Moderately Effective*	*Somewhat Effective*	*Not Too Effective*	*Scrap the Suggestion*

if it is to be effective, must fill the community's expectations. Often, educators assume they know what the community wants. This leads to faulty communication and eventual resentment.

Second, community members provide constructive strategies for the creation of a safe school environment. Community members have an array of experience. These experiences, although different from those of educators, provide the means to develop breakthrough paradigms in constructing effective strategies.

Third, team members learn to become culturally literate. They are able to put ideas into a context that are acceptable to the community. Because team members understand the community's culture, they identify the community's patterns of acting, inherent beliefs, and values.

Strategy that does not integrate the community's culture is destined to fail. For example, school board members in a city in the Northeast had to make a decision as to whether they should build two large high schools or a mega–high school campus. The community's intense pride in their athletic teams made this a difficult decision. The community resisted educator attempts to build two high schools. Educators were unable to convince the community that the educational reasons for two campuses outweighed the benefits of maintaining a dominant athletic program. The community's resistance was so forceful that the school board built a single high school housing more than four thousand students. Once the school leader and team identify and understand the community's culture, they can develop an aligning strategy.

Community involvement is a critical component to aligning strategy. Effective strategy development is a grassroots process that builds partnerships between the school and the community. The community has a personal stake in creating safe schools. Its commitment to a safe school strategy will be directly proportional to the community's level of meaningful involvement.

FRAMING THE ISSUE

Teachers, students, parents, and community members have different ways of interpreting what they see. These different interpretations are *frames*. Because each group has a different frame, consensus is often difficult. Identifying these frames and understanding them leads to consensus. Discovering common ground among the array of frames allows the school leader to describe the components of the safe school plan in a way that facilitates understanding by members of each group.

Framing does not change the issue. It changes the view when looking at an issue. When we frame an object, we fit it to hold certain dimensions. Imagine you are looking through a camera lens at a landscape. The lens provides you with a frame of the landscape, not a view of the entire landscape. If you want to take a picture of the landscape to communicate this landscape, you choose a frame that represents the entire landscape. Similarly, when the school leader and her team want to communicate their safe school plan to the community, they need to frame their communication for the school community. In effect, when we frame strategy we shape attitudes.

Attitudes are the mental processes that people use to respond to external stimuli. In effect, our attitude shapes our behavior. Conversely, our behavior shapes our attitude.[14] Understanding the relationship between attitude and behavior allows the effective school leader to use framing to elicit a constructive attitude toward the team's safe school plans.

Maria Peterson, a high school principal, understood the principle of framing. She wanted her teachers to handle the majority of classroom discipline issues though she knew they would resist handling all such problems. Instead, Maria framed the issue by suggesting that prevention was the key to creating an effective learning environment. Her framing strategy and attitude empowered teachers. Teachers viewed Maria's efforts as focusing on instruction rather than discipline management. Maria is a skilled performer when it comes to framing issues. Framing is an important skill that school leaders can develop.

The school leader encourages team members to practice framing so that they can communicate the safe school plan to the community. For practice, change the negative frame of the following four items to a positive frame:

1. The school board is constantly prying into the school's activities.
2. Some parent groups in the district are overly aggressive.

3. Teachers in the district are demanding a greater say in school governance.
4. The resources for effective education in this community are not available.

We can frame these issues into optimistic, positive reference points. For example, team members at one middle school chose to reframe "The school board is constantly prying into the school's activities" into "The community's school board is actively involved in the educational process." The school leader, by framing issues into optimistic, positive reference points, defuses defensiveness resulting from different value systems. This action by the school leader also empowers members of the school community.

COMPONENTS OF A WELL-WRITTEN SAFE SCHOOL PLAN

Two elements are particularly important for an effective plan for safe schools.

An Effective Safe School Plan Has a Clear Statement of the Problem

The school leader, by clearly stating problems, eliminates ambiguity and confusion. A clearly stated problem provides team members with an unmistakable focus. An effective safe school plan relates directly to the school's metaphor. The safe school plan becomes one of the operational components moving the school community toward full identification with the metaphor. An effective safe school plan is inclusive and designed to bring people together in a common cause.

Effective safe school plans focus on the systemic causes and sources of the identified problems. It identifies the internal causes and sources of problems as the first place to focus an effective strategy. These plans aim at the source of a problem as the most effective place to initiate change. It does this by providing multiple options that are measured against well-defined criteria. Each of these criteria meets high standards. When the developed safe school plan meets these standards, it serves as a source of commitment for the school community. Commitment deepens when members consensually agree to each aspect of the safe school plan. They realize that the safe school plan embodies common shared values of the school community.

An Effective Safe School Plan Identifies Appropriate Tactics

A *tactic* is a set of actions to secure an end, aim, or a mission. A tactic provides the means to an end. Like the strategy, the school leader and team align tactics with the school community's values. The safe school plan links shared values with appropriate tactics. Each value connects to a tactic. The connections between shared values and tactics are clearly identifiable. The most effective tactics have their foundation in the shared values of the school community. For example, corporal punishment is one tactic still advocated in some communities. In other communities, corporal punishment is unacceptable. The community must value the tactic or the tactic detracts from the overall strategy.

Each tactic connects to a specific knowledge base. Linking tactics to a knowledge base gives the school leader information and knowledge-based power. The effective school leader links tactics to sound theoretical, psychological, and pedagogical educational theories. In addition, the effective school leader adapts successful tactics implemented in other schools. Adding successful tactics implemented in other schools adds credibility to the overall strategy.

COMMUNICATING THE SAFE SCHOOL PLAN

The effective school leader communicates the safe school plan by integrating it into the school community's vocabulary. The goal of communication is to build a deep sense of commitment to the plan. Impelling communication has its source in each team member's belief that the safe school plan is tenable, applicable, and viable. Harry Adler, a neurolinguistic programming expert, states:

> In communicating, either in words, gestures or overall body language, we are seeking to get nearer to the "territory" of reality, but, more practically, we are trying to bridge the gap between our map of what is real and the map of the other person. Consequently, congruence between maps, or perceptions, and the transfer of understanding, rather than the futile quest for "reality," is our objective. And this is how we need to approach communication.[15]

When the community understands and supports the strategy, tactics, and desired outcomes of the safe school plan, the school leader knows that he has successfully communicated the safe school plan.

SUMMARY

This chapter describes the power of the belief system, importance of commitment, team confidence, and essential components of a safe school plan. The belief system focuses on the importance of personal and organizational beliefs. It describes how to identify limiting beliefs and how to replace limiting beliefs with empowering beliefs. The belief system resembles a triangle having three essential components: the leader, the members of the community, and a collaboratively developed prescription. There is a synergy between the leader and the school community members in which each expresses confidence in each other. The belief triangle supports the leader and school community members. It creates a synergistic effect that produces success. Generating commitment to a common cause is essential to the development of an effective safe school environment. Commitment begins with the school leader and team developing confidence in each other that each has the capacity to contribute to a successful outcome. The confidence that the school leader and team members

Putting It Together: Advancing with Vigilance	✓
Does everyone understand the power of the belief system? Has everyone identified limiting beliefs and replaced them with empowering beliefs? Does the school team have a sense of confidence in constructing a safe school environment? Does the school team have a sense of personal competence that each member has the skills to contribute to the construction of a safe school environment? Is the community involved in sharing ideas regarding problems and potential solutions? Has the school team identified and understood the community's culture? Has the team conceptualized effective ways to frame the safe school plan to the community? Are there mutual belief and respect between the leader and the members? Have members shared ideas? Does the team understand the crucial components to writing an effective safe school plan?	

have in each other affects the entire school community. The school community, sensing this high level of confidence, more willingly embraces emerging strategies and tactics that the team recommends as part of its overall safe school plan.

NOTES

1. David Sobel and Robert Ornstein, *The Healthy Mind Healthy Body Handbook* (New York: Patient Education Media, 1996), 41.
2. "Characteristics of Leaders of Change," Southwest Educational Development Laboratory (1999), <http://www.sedl.org/change/leadership/character.html> (28 March 2000).
3. Anthony Robbins, *Awaken the Giant Within* (New York: Fireside Books, 1991), 73.
4. Robert Dilts, Tim Hallbom, and Suzi Smith, *Beliefs: Pathways to Health and Well-being* (Portland, Ore.: Metamorphous, 1990), 3.
5. "Implications for Leaders of School Improvement," Southwest Educational Development Laboratory (1999), <http://www.sedl.org/change/school/implications.html> (28 March 2000).
6. Herbert Benson, *Timeless Healing: The Power and Biology of Belief* (New York: Scribner, 1996), 63.
7. Sharon S. Brehm and Saul M. Kassin, "Foundations of Perception," in *Psychological Dimensions of Organizational Behavior*, ed. Barry Straw (New York: Maxwell Macmillan, 1991), 199.
8. Roger Schank, *Tell Me a Story* (New York: Scribner's, 1990), xi–xii.
9. "History of Leadership Research," Southwest Educational Development Laboratory (1999), <http://www.sedl.org/change/leadership/history.html> (28 March 2000).
10. Dilts et al., *Beliefs: Pathways to Health and Well-being*.
11. Charles Garfield, *Peak Performance* (New York: Warner Books, 1984), 34.
12. Warren Bennis, "Transformative Power and Leadership," in *Leadership and Organization Culture*, ed. Thomas J. Sergiovanni and John Corbally (Urbana: University of Illinois Press, 1984), 64–71.
13. Ann T. Lockwood, "Comprehensive Reform: A Guide for School Leaders," *Leaders for Tomorrow's Schools* (Spring 1998), <http://www.ncrel.org/cscd/pubs/lead52/52three.htm> (28 June 2000).
14. Andrew Goliszek, *Breaking the Stress Habit: A Modern Guide to One-Minute Stress Management* (Winston-Salem, N.C.: Carolina Press, 1987).
15. Harry Adler, *NLP for Trainers: Communicating for Excellence* (New York: McGraw-Hill, 1996), 50.

CHAPTER FIVE

Apply Appropriate Actions

Constructing an effective safe school environment requires using appropriate actions. Using appropriate actions contributes to the effective implementation of a safe school strategy. Imagine an artist contemplating a block of marble. The block of marble has potential to transform into a great work. However, the block of marble is only potential. It needs the artist to transform the block of marble into a masterpiece. The artist, using the chisel and other sculpturing devices, applies his craft. The artist's actions, applied accurately, transform the block of marble from a formless object into a meaningful work of art. Similarly, the actions provided in this chapter transform the safe school plan into reality. Actions are the instrumental means that achieve constructive outcomes. The effective school leader, in conjunction with her team, applies appropriate actions to ensure the success of the strategic safe school plan.

In this chapter, you will

- understand how to link the vision to the safe school strategy,
- learn how to link the mission to the safe school strategy,
- understand how to tie a SWOT analysis to the existing school environment, and
- understand how to connect appropriate benchmarks to the safe school strategy.

LINKING THE TEAM'S VISION TO THE SAFE SCHOOL PLAN

The first action is to link the team's vision to the safe school plan. A vision is essential to any creative process. *Vision* is a frequently misunderstood term. A. Lorri Manasse, an educational researcher, states that a vision is "the force which molds meaning for the people of an organization."[1] Vision is one of the building blocks of leadership. Without it, a group, unit, or person wanders aimlessly. The person or group has no destination, no compelling reason for moving from a present position to another, and much different position.

Developing a vision requires effort. Management consultant Tom Peters provides eight requirements for an effective vision. Effective visions

- inspire,
- challenge,
- endure,
- have flexibility,
- act as beacons,
- empower members of the group,
- honor the past, and
- are detailed.[2]

COMPONENTS OF AN EFFECTIVE VISION

Developing a shared vision entails four components: knowing your context, involving essential players, seeing the future, and committing it to writing.[3] A vision relates to the community and its context. The vision is also collaboratively developed by members with a personal stake in the organization. These members remain in the organization's contextual influence long after the leadership changes. This vision has a compelling sense of the future. It is a vision of aspiration. Aspiration provides a compelling sense and requisite energy needed by the organization to embark on its journey. This compelling and aspiring vision, when committed to writing, becomes a reference and rallying point for members of the organization.

Effective visions have similar characteristics. The North Central Regional Educational Laboratory cites five components of an effective vision:[4]

1. The vision needs to be achievable. The members of the team and the school community have to believe that the vision is attainable.
2. The vision needs alignment with the school community's shared values. The shared values are the vision's fuel and act as an inclusive community-building agent.

3. The vision must be a cogent representation of what the school will be like in the future. In effect, it applies a magnetic drawing power focusing the energy and interests of the members of the school community on collaborative outcome.
4. When translated into action, the vision moves from a state of potential energy to one of kinetic energy. It engages a defined process whose objective is the attainment of the vision.
5. The vision, when communicated to the members of the school community, builds bonds between members of the safe school team and members of the school community.

The vision rises out of full participation in its genesis. Ed Oakley and Doug Krug, in *Enlightened Leadership,* state, "Going through the process of defining a mission or vision encourages people to clarify both their organizational and individual values. The process has them clarify what is important to them and how what they want can be achieved through achieving the organization's vision."[5]

The school leader, in generating a vision, has team members brainstorm descriptions of the school's future identity. Descriptions are clear and concise to prevent ambiguity in understanding. The following are examples of clear and concise descriptions:

- The school is safe.
- Classrooms are learning environments.
- Teachers and students respect each other.

The school leader, in facilitating this process, writes each description inside a large circle. The circle becomes symbolic of inclusion. Terms inside the circle symbolically inform members that there is room for an array of descriptions. Each description draws the team closer to its vision. Burt Nanus, management and leadership expert, says, "Vision is a realistic, credible, attractive future for your organization. It is your articulation of a destination toward which your organization should aim, a future that in important ways is better, more successful or more desirable for your organization than is the present."[6] Descriptions that result in this type of vision will empower your school and its members.

A powerful vision statement is simple. It communicates a sense of destination. It communicates a sense of power, belief, energy, and above all a hope. Figure 5.1 represents an excellent vision statement.

JONES MIDDLE SCHOOL IS A PLCE WHERE STUDENTS, TEACHERS,

PARENTS, AND ADMINISTRATORS GATHER IN MUTUAL RESPECT.

TOGETHER, THEY PROMOTE SAFETY, LEARNING, AND SOCIAL GROWTH.

IT IS A DEMOCRATIC SCHOOL REPRESENTING THE NEEDS AND

ASPIRATIONS OF ALL MEMBERS.

Figure 5.1   Vision Statement

This vision statement tells us that Jones Middle School has a clear indication of its destination. Its vision statement is clear, concise, and complete. However, even with a powerful vision, the vision is powerless without commitment to the vision. Commitment to a vision is the difference between managing and leading. The school team must take the responsibility for building commitment among community members. As the school team builds commitment to the vision among community members, the vision empowers and transforms the school organization. Peter Senge, MIT management authority, states, "Most people have goals and objectives, but no sense of a real vision. Vision differs from purpose. Vision is a definite picture of a desired future, while purpose is more abstract. But vision without a sense of purpose is equally futile."[7] It is this sense of vision that energizes people and transforms organizations.

A principal of a northeastern high school described a clear vision of his school. He said that he saw a school (and still sees it today) where students respect teachers, teachers respect students, learning is paramount, there is a sense of order in classrooms and halls, and civility governs discourse. The principal led a drug- and violence-free school. This principal consistently monitored the progress toward his vision. He knew when the school was moving toward the vision or when it was moving away from the vision. It was that vision that steered the principal to organize his faculty, administrators, and students to work toward a safe school promoting a learning environment. This principal carried that vision wherever he went. He explained the vision consistently to his faculty, students, and parents. Everyone was clear as to the school's destination and direction. There were no doubts about direction. One could look at the map and see the school's final destination. The school community embraced the principal's vision. It served the underlying motivation that brought the school community together. This principal was able to construct and apply a vision that fills the function of vision as described by Bennis and Nanus. These two leadership and management experts state:

> To choose a direction, a leader must first have developed a mental image of a possible and desirable future state of the organization. This image, which we call a vision, may be as vague as a dream or as precise as a goal or mission statement. The critical point is that a vision articulates a view of a realistic, credible, attractive future for the organization, a condition that is better in some important ways than what now exists.[8]

THE TEAM'S MISSION AS A MEANS TO ACHIEVING A VISION

The second action is to develop a mission that moves the school community toward its vision. "*Mission* comes from the Latin word *mittere*, meaning 'to throw, let go, or send.' Also derived from Latin, the word *purpose* meant to declare. Whether you call it a mission or purpose, it represents the fundamental reason for the organization's existence."[9] The mission of the school is more action oriented than the vision. A vision is abstract. To reach a destination, the members of the organization need a mission or a series of missions. Seldom does a single mission bring the group to its final destination. Each mission, carefully plotted, brings the group or organization closer to its ultimate destination. A mission has a specific purpose. Its goals and objectives are clear. The mission moves the organization from its point of origin to its point of destination. This concept is applicable to all organizations.

The school leader takes responsibility for moving the school from its point of origin to its point of destination. This is the school leader's mission. The school leader, in pursuing this mission, communicates a sense of urgency, responsibility, and energy. The following are clear and concise mission statements: "Our mission is to reduce the number of students who drop out of school." "Our mission is to raise student achievement scores." These mission statements are clear, short, and concise. Each person understands his or her responsibility and the organization's direction. When the mission is nebulous, there is confusion over organizational priorities and purpose.

An effective mission creates a sense of focus. Successful people and organizations have a clear focus. *Focus* is the ability to discard distractions. It is the ability to set clear, identifiable, and attainable priorities.

Mission statements also are flexible. They change as circumstances change. However, as they change to adapt to dynamic environments, the mission statement maintains its same sense of urgency, responsibility, and energy.

Excellent organizations have brief mission statements. Confused organizations have large and rambling mission statements that fail to communicate a sense of urgency, responsibility, or energy.

According to James Barker:

> Because of its set of traditional values, employees give the mission statement legitimacy and feel obligated and expected to act according to its tenants. Through their actions, they internalize the "traditional" authority of the mission statement. They take ownership of these corporate values and begin to develop their own sets of values to guide their collective actions on the team.[10]

The development of a mission statement powers the vision. It is a statement of responsibility and commitment. It becomes the school's persona.

MISSIONS ACT AS GUIDEPOSTS

The school leader needs to create a route between his school's point of origin and destination point. As he creates this route, he determines essential guideposts leading to the destination. Guideposts are strategic places to rest, reflect, and reorient. The distance between each guidepost represents a separate mission. The school leader and his team successfully complete a mission when they arrive at each succeeding guidepost.

The first mission statement takes the team from the point of origin to its first guidepost. The route to the final point of destination zigzags. The dynamic nature of the environment influences the route, and the school leader is aware that the only predictable constant is change. John Gardner, leadership authority, states, "We were designed for struggle, for survival. Only fatal and final injuries neutralize that irrepressible striving toward the light an older deeply rooted, biologically and spiritually stubborn part of us continues to say yes to hoping, yes to striving, yes to life."[11] This is the dynamic nature of mission where there is no certitude, only challenge.

The dynamic nature of the environment differs from one school to the next, from one organization to the next. One community provides schools with a clear set of mandates regarding education. The types of issues in this community are far different from a community where there is no such mandate. The mission in the former community may be "Every student in this year's senior class will be accepted into college." The primary mission in the latter community may be "Acts of violence and drug abuse will be eliminated from our campus." These two different schools have two different contexts resulting in two different mission statements.

When the school accomplishes the mission, the school leader and her team formulate a new mission. In the previous example, once the school eliminates acts of violence and drug dealing, a new mission emerges. This mission statement may become "We will raise achievement scores among ninth grade students." The successful completion of each mission brings the school closer to reaching its vision. In large organizations, simultaneous missions coexist. A school may have missions focused on discipline, student achievement, and teacher professional growth. These are simultaneous missions, occurring at any given time, with each pointing toward the final destination.

As the school leader and her team develop their mission statements, the school leader is aware that the maximum amount of pieces of information members can successfully process at a time is 7 ± 2. Once members exceed that limit, information overload occurs, and the system becomes dysfunctional. Imagine a juggler juggling three balls. The juggler adds another ball (four balls now) and another (five). As the number of balls increases, the juggler's hands move faster and faster. The juggler watches the five balls in the air. The juggler adds another (six) and then another (seven). The juggler is nearly at maximum in terms of the amount of balls to maintain at any given time. The juggler adds another ball (eight) and another (nine). The juggler's hands are moving so quickly that one can hardly see them move. Finally, the juggler adds the tenth ball. The ten balls come crashing to the ground. This is what happens in organizations when administrators fail to consider the maximum number of tasks or amounts of information employees can effectively manage.

CREATE A MAP

The mission is the map. The wagon master's first mission is to organize the wagon train. Once the wagon master organizes the wagon train, he has to get the wagon train across the Mississippi River. After the members of the wagon train accomplish each mission, the wagon master identifies a new mission. Similarly, the school team identifies the necessary steps from the point of origin to the point of destination. Each step is a point on a map.

The school leader lists each mission that must take place for the team to reach the point of destination. Once the school leader identifies the mission, the team shares the mission with members of the school community. Successful missions have a buy-in by the members of the school community. Therefore, the school leader's task is to motivate and inspire each member of the school community to embrace the mission. To the extent that there is widespread cooperation, goals are achieved, missions are completed, and the vision is attained. Even with a clear map, the mission needs to be empowered. The power comes from goals.

Goals supply the power to the mission. Motivation increases when members are aware of the benefits they will gain if they commit to the goals associated with the mission. The personal benefits that people recognize coming forth from the goals are their primary source of motivation. The school leader and her team identify benefits and communicate them to the school community. The school communicates the costs associated with the mission in terms of personal effort, time, and emotional investment. The leader identifies the costs associated with the goals and mission. An effective school leader knows that the benefits have to outweigh the costs to gain commitment from team members and the school community. The following equation demonstrates the importance of focusing on benefits and costs in gaining commitment:

$$\text{Benefits} - \text{Costs} = \text{Level of Commitment}$$

The effective school leader and his team communicate the benefits of the safe school plan to the members of the school community. The trust developed by the school leader and his team reinforces the veracity of the benefits they espouse. Without trust, the school community will not believe the benefits are real. Trust is the critical component to this process. When the school community identifies with the benefits in embracing the mission, they will cooperate to complete each mission and work toward achieving the vision.

THE SWOT ANALYSIS AS A MEANS TO UNDERSTANDING THE ENVIRONMENTAL CONTEXT

A vision and mission are critical to the school organization in its strategic planning to develop an effective safe school plan. The effectiveness of the vision and its mission correlates, in large part, to the school team's ability to access its current condition accurately. The third action, a SWOT analysis, allows the school team to assess the current condition of the school.

The SWOT analysis is a tool that allows the school team to determine its point of origin. A SWOT analysis looks at four major organizational components:

S = Strengths
W = Weaknesses
O = Opportunities
T = Threats

Strengths

Strengths refer to the current effective strategies that address instructional, safety, cultural, and social issues. An effective strategy may be the classroom management skills employed by teachers. Another effective strategy may be excellent teacher and parent communication processes. A third effective strategy may be the school administration's compilation and use of a database on discipline or instructional issues. The school leader determines strengths by identifying and evaluating existing strategies and tactics. The school leader and team evaluate strategies and tactics by collecting evidence that documents effectiveness. One example of a strength is the booklet explaining the "rules for student behavior" at Centennial High School in Portland, Oregon. All parents and students understand the school's requirements for student conduct.[12] This booklet is part of an overall effective safe school strategy employed at Centennial High School.

Weaknesses

Weaknesses refer to the ineffectiveness of current strategies and tactics in addressing safe school issues; they refer to strategies and tactics, not people. Some examples of weaknesses include these:

- Lack of administrative follow-up
- Low performance by students on state achievement tests destroys the teacher and student confidence

- High number of teacher discipline referrals to the office
- Lack of teacher–parent communication
- Lack of administrator–parent communication
- The lack of school board support
- Lack of a database of discipline problems
- Negative teacher attitudes toward students
- Unwillingness of teachers to monitor student attendance during classes

Judgment of a weakness requires an identified outcome or standard. The school leader and her team use high standards of schools with programs to identify weaknesses in current programs (see Table 5.1).

Identifying weaknesses, as part of the SWOT process, requires a complete examination of safe school strategies. It is similar to a physical examination that a patient receives from a doctor. The patient wants her doctor to screen for potential health hazards. She wants the doctor to tell her the truth. Healthy people maintain their health by addressing problem

Table 5.1 Effective School Discipline Standards[13]

Standard Number	Preventive Discipline Method
Method 1: Commitment	Commitment on the part of the school community to establish and sustain suitable student conduct is a prerequisite to learning.
Method 2: Clear and broad-based standards for behavior	Clear and broad-based standards for behavior. The school's rules, sanctions, and actions have input from students. They are understandable and widely communicated.
Method 3: Warm school climate	Create a warm social climate characterized by a concern for students as individuals. Teachers and administrators take an interest in the personal goals, achievements, and problems of students and support them in their academic and extracurricular activities.
Method 4: Visible, supportive administrators	Principals are visible in hallways and classrooms, talking informally with teachers and students, speaking to them by name, and expressing interest in their activities.
Method 5: Delegation of discipline authority to teachers	Teachers handle routine classroom discipline problems.
Method 6: Community connections	High levels of parent–school interaction exist. The community participates in goal setting and achievement of school-related goals.
Method 7: High expectations	Teachers and administrators set high expectations for student behavior.

areas and modifying behaviors to regain and maintain personal health. It is the same way with organizations. Periodic self-examinations of strengths and weaknesses are critical to any healthy organization.

Opportunities

The school leader and his team list the potential opportunities coming from the successful implementation of the safe school plan. The identification of opportunities serves as motivational benchmarks for an organization. Opportunities come in different formats. For example, the identification by the state as a high performance school and identification as a model for other schools are recognitions that can create significant opportunities. These opportunities may appear as significantly higher morale, new partnerships between parents and teachers, the attraction of greater resources, and increased numbers of graduates attending college. One middle school sought and received recognition of its creative discipline program in a Phi Delta Kappan publication as a school with exemplary discipline.[14] This was a motivating tool for faculty and students. It resulted in being a source of pride for parents, administrators, teachers, and students. Opportunities are limitless when the school leader and team brainstorm the possibilities.

Threats

Team members need to list existing threats to their school. A threat is an event that has the potential to occur. Examples of contemporary threats to schools include terrorist attacks, kidnappings, hostage situations, extreme violence, and public suicide by teachers or students. Every person connected with the school and surrounding community possesses the potential to be a threat. Some threats to schools come from fringe groups outside the awareness of the school leader and members of the school community. When threats realize their potential, the entire school and community suffer. The following history of threats that realized their potential demonstrates the crucial nature of this SWOT characteristic.

Feb. 2, 1996, Moses Lake, Washington, two students and one teacher killed, one other wounded when 14-year-old Barry Loukaitis opened fire on his algebra class.

Feb. 19, 1997, Bethel, Alaska, principal and one student killed, two others wounded by Evan Ramsey, 16, at his high school.

Oct. 1, 1997, Pearl, Mississippi, 2 students killed and 7 wounded by a 16-year-old who was also accused of killing his mother. He and several friends thought to be in on the plot were said to be outcasts who worshipped Satan.

Dec. 1, 1997, West Paducah, Kentucky, three students killed, five wounded by a 14-year-old boy as they participated in a prayer circle at Heath High School.

Dec. 15, 1997, Stamps, Arkansas, 2 students wounded. Colt Todd, 14, was hiding in the woods when he shot the students as they stood in the parking lot.

March 24, 1998, Jonesboro, Arkansas, four students and one teacher killed, 10 others wounded outside as Westside Middle School emptied during a false fire alarm. Mitchell Johnson, 13, and Andrew Golden, 11, shot at their classmates and teachers from the woods.

April 24, 1998, Edinboro, Pennsylvania, one teacher killed, two students wounded at a dance at James W. Parker Middle School. A 14-year-old boy was charged.

May 19, 1998, Fayetteville, Tennessee, 1 student killed in the parking lot at Lincoln County High School three days before he was to graduate. The victim was dating the ex-girlfriend of his killer, 18-year-old honor student Jacob Davis.

May 21, 1998, Springfield, Oregon, two students killed, 22 others wounded in the cafeteria at Thurston High School by 15-year-old Kip Kinkel. Kinkel had been arrested and released to his parents a day earlier, after it was discovered that he had a gun at school. His parents were later found dead at home.

June 15, 1998, Richmond, Virginia, 1 teacher and 1 guidance counselor wounded by a 14-year-old boy in the hallway of a Richmond high school.

April 20, 1999, Littleton, Colorado, 14 students (including killers) and 1 teacher killed, 23 others wounded at Columbine High School in the nation's deadliest school shooting. Eric Harris, 18, and Dylan Klebold, 17, had plotted for a year to kill at least 500 and blow up their school. At the end of their hour-long rampage, they turned their guns on themselves.

April 28, 1999, Taber, Alberta, Canada, one student killed, one wounded at W. R. Myers High School in first fatal high school shooting in Canada in 20 years. The suspect, a 14-year-old boy, had been unhappy at Myers and dropped out in order to begin home schooling.

May 20, 1999, Conyers, Georgia, 6 students injured at Heritage High School by 15-year-old T. J. Solomon, who was reportedly depressed after breaking up with his girlfriend.

Dec. 6, 1999, Fort Gibson, Oklahoma, 4 students wounded and 1 severely bruised in the chaos as a 13-year-old boy opened fire with a 9mm semi-automatic handgun at Fort Gibson Middle School.

Feb. 2, 2000, Derik Lehman, a 17-year-old at Royal Palm Beach High School, expelled from school and placed on house arrest after making threats to a killing spree at his school.

April 20, 2000, Ashley Smith, a 15-year-old Palm Beach Lakes High School freshman, threatened to bomb his school on the Columbine anniversary.

May 26, 2000, Barry Grunow, a 35-year-old teacher at Lake Worth Middle School, shot in the face by seventh-grader Nathaniel Brazill, 13, on the last day of school.[15]

Modified SWOT Analysis

The completion of the SWOT analysis gives the school leader and his school team a clear picture of the school's point of origin. Now it has potential application to assess the status of academic performance, community support, or any other point of origin and provides community members an opportunity to express concerns and gain a balanced view of current conditions. After completing the SWOT analysis, the school leader and his team work with smaller groups within the school community to share their findings and seek feedback on potential gaps in the analysis. This is an effective strategy to discover new strengths, threats, opportunities, and weaknesses. Figure 5.2 shows a modified SWOT analysis.

IDENTIFY AND APPLY APPROPRIATE BENCHMARKS

Benchmarking is a critical tool to identify excellent practices as the standard for success. Private industry applies the principles of benchmarking to improve product performance and capture greater market share. "Benchmarking entails comparing performances to best practices from within and outside your [school], and using the results as a basis for action. It directs attention outward to best practices and helps set goals for improvement. The targets come from what others have done in practice."[16]

Many educators confuse benchmarking with checkpoints. *Checkpoints* gauge the distance one has traveled from the source. They act as indicators of progress in the correct direction to reach the point of destination. They signal mission completion. Benchmarking compares organizational growth against the best practices in the world. It is a means of constantly seeking and then maintaining optimum quality.

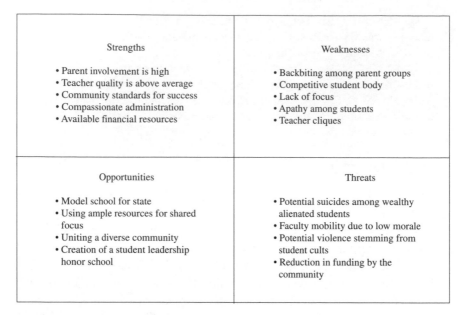

Figure 5.2   SWOT Analysis

Using appropriate benchmarks is a source of motivation for members of the school community. The effective school leader aligns the safe school plan with the best models that exist. In this way, the school leader and her team constantly strive for improved performance. There is no resting on achievements by the school community. The ultimate goal is to surpass existing benchmarks and become the benchmark for other schools.

There are four types of benchmarks:

1. Organizational benchmarking
2. Competitive benchmarking
3. Unilateral benchmarking
4. Futuristic benchmarking

Organizational Benchmarking

Organizational benchmarking refer to benchmarks within the school's organizational environment. For example, Damm Middle School belongs to a much larger organization, the school district. The principal of Damm Middle School wants to consider the best practices in use at the other district schools, so she compares the practices: the number of suspensions, acts of reported violence, teacher referrals to the office, number of phone calls between teachers and parents, increase in student performance, and number of students committed to working in community service projects. It is important to measure apples with apples and oranges with oranges when benchmarking.

Competitive Benchmarking

Competitive benchmarking identifies best practices in and external to the education profession. It serves as a rallying point for parents, teachers, and students. Many educators tell their teachers, students, and parents that they can be the best. However, being the best means willingness to match current performance against the performance levels of the best schools. This can be a source of motivation. Once the school becomes the best in the district, then the school leadership team can seek to become the best in a region, then best in the state, then best in the nation. It is a continual source of motivation and pride.

Often, people fear comparisons. Teachers in a low-income urban school, for example, may fear comparisons with a school in an affluent environment. However, research demonstrates that children from poor urban environments can compete with students from high socioeconomic environments. Marva Collins in Chicago and Jaime Escalante in Los Angeles set benchmarks with inner-city youth.

Unilateral Benchmarking

Unilateral benchmarking seeks out the best possible practices despite the profession. When the school team employs unilateral benchmarking, the team moves beyond the scope of traditional circles in identifying best practices. The school team considers practices in private schools, juvenile detention facilities, or private industry. The school team identifies models of excellence and then copies these models precisely, adapting them to their environment. For example, a team may identify a juvenile detention facility where adolescents have extremely low rates of recidivism and learn to become outstanding citizens. The training in that facility may be a model to emulate.

Futuristic Benchmarking

Futuristic benchmarking examines the trends expected to emerge in the future. These trends will have a major impact on adolescents, parent relations, curriculum, organization, academics, and teacher development. The Northwest Regional Educational Laboratory identifies twelve trends expected to affect education:

1. Renewed focus on curriculum and instruction
2. Increased emphasis on standards and accountability
3. Enrollments of minority, poor, and special education students will increase
4. Instability and unpredictable resource allocation
5. Changing roles in school and community decision making
6. Increased disparity between rich and poor communities
7. Increased state involvement in local education decisions
8. Increased competition for existing public funds
9. Increased demands by the public for greater participation in the educational process
10. Increased integration of available service to meet the needs of children
11. The gap between rich and poor families will increase
12. Barriers related to full achievement for all students will remain[17]

Strategic safe school planning considers future trends. The trends that affect schools in California will affect schools in Rhode Island. Isolation and size do not protect the school community. Global communication links small communities with large communities, people in China with those in Utah, and principals in Russia with those in the United States.

POTENTIAL EMERGING BENCHMARKS

Potential emerging benchmarks are influenced by the rapid advances of technology.

Rapid Advances of Technology and the Impact of Technology within the Classroom

Classroom management skills will be different. Students will work independently as opposed to working in groups. Some teachers will no longer stand in front of class lecturing; they will move from desk to desk as they monitor student performance at computer stations. Other teachers will provide satellite instruction or instruction over the Internet to their students. Teachers will use technical skills such as Power Point and other strategies to develop and transmit lessons to students. As technology gains further dominance in the instructional process, teachers will act as learning coaches, guiding, pacing, and measuring individual student performance. General classroom distractions will not be as pronounced as in the past. On the other hand, teachers will be more concerned with damage to equipment and student abuse of the World Wide Web. The close personal relationship formed by teacher and student in this emerging pattern will require school leaders to do detailed background checks on any potential hire.

New Forms of Technology and Communication

The technology age will allow school administrators, teachers, counselors, and other personnel to communicate instantly with parents. Many schools are using e-mail messages, pagers, and cellular phones to communicate with parents. Within a short time, e-mail will be archaic and replaced by new, yet rapidly developing, communication technology. Effective school leaders are alert to developments in communication and creatively explore ways that these forms of communication strengthen the relationship between school and parents. Effective school leaders will use this technology to apprise parents continually of potential problems and allow the parents to assume a partnership role with teachers and administrators.

Expansion of the School Context

Many students will learn in multiple alternative environments managed by the school. These alternative environments, for example, may include a small center in their neighborhood or a job environment. The school will be the hub for learning that extends into a variety of learning environments. School leaders, depending on the level of supervision, may be responsible for student safety in these environments. School leaders will evaluate the site and people involved in those sites as a primary step in protecting their students and teachers.

Small-Group Meetings in the Community

School officials will meet with parents in small groups in the parents' neighborhood. These small-group meetings will serve as a vehicle for communicating and improving parents' interest in their child's progress. They will also serve to facilitate the continuous training of parents, especially those parents whose backgrounds are limited due to social and environmental circumstances. Moving the learning environment from the school into neighborhoods and homes creates greater trust of school officials by parents. This is an important strategy in environments where there has been little historical trust of public authority figures. The decentralization of schooling allows effective school administrators to build bridges of trust with parents.

Increased School Oversight Options

Regional, state, and national government agencies will monitor schools.

- They will identify high- or low-performing schools based on achievement test results.
- They will closely monitor issues of equity and fairness.
- They will monitor dropout rates, suspension rates, and graduation rates based on race, ethnicity, and gender.
- They will set performance goals with little involvement of local administrators.

Administrators and teachers who identify these performance trends and proactively respond before performance levels are set will position their school for success.

CREATING BENCHMARKS

Effective school leaders involve the school community in the benchmarking process. Involving members of the school community allows the linking of benchmarks to essential community goals. One community, for example, has an investment in keeping students off the street during traditional working hours. This is a police-driven goal to eliminate daytime burglaries. This community, by using this benchmark, is looking at ideal practices about in-school suspensions and other alternative models to suspensions.

The school leader identifies the models or prototypes to use for the benchmarking process. Once she identifies appropriate models, she visits the people who developed the model. Not only does she want to view the actual operation of the benchmark model, she needs to discover how the various components of the model fit together. She needs to become aware of attitudes of teachers, students, parents, and administrators to the model. She will need to detect the minute intricacies that the benchmarking group has put into place to make their model effective. In effect, the school leader is identifying each component of the benchmarking model.

The school leader accurately identifies the components of the benchmark program by applying the following questions to this process:

1. What were the problems that motivated you to consider this model?
2. How did you develop this model?
3. Who are the essential players in implementing this model?
4. How did you gain teacher agreement?
5. How did you get the students to respond favorably to the model?
6. How are parents involved in this model?
7. What types of training did you use to get teachers, staff, parents, and students ready for this model?
8. Who were the trainers for this model?
9. How long did it take to implement the model?

To identify how the selected benchmark models adapt to your environment, the team has to see the benchmark model fitting into their metaphor, vision, and applicable missions. The school team must understand, explain, and communicate the benefits of the benchmark model to other members of the school community. The team has to demonstrate why the model is the benchmark your school will set as a standard. This process informs the community that the school leader and his team will not settle for anything less than the best performance.

Once the school leader and team select a benchmark program, they apply the strategy of chunking. *Chunking* is a term used in the private sector that means to break things down to manageable size. In using the benchmarking process, teams and leaders chunk a model down to a strategic trial size and implement it on a small scale. The team can evaluate it over a course of six to ten weeks. At the end of the trial phase, the team determines how this smaller version works and whether they should continue or expand the model. Too many schools fall into the bandwagon syndrome. They hear of a good practice, adopt it without a trial process, and then look for another practice. This is poor practice. The planning process eliminates poor practice and places your school strategically at the front of all other schools for adopting and adapting solid, substantive practices.

Benefits of Benchmarking

Significant benefits accrue to schools that use the benchmarking process. The first is an increase in chance for success. The effective school leader uses the best-known practices in his field and adjacent fields. Think of the power this provides to the school leader when he communicates with the school board and community. He is using the best practices, he understands these practices, and he has chosen them because they are effective in similar environments.

The second benefit of benchmarking is that it overcomes resistance to change. The school community will more readily accept proposals because they are best practices. There will be few substantive arguments against adopting best practices. If arguments against adapting the identified model do arise, the best strategy is to ask those in opposition to provide the team with a substitute model of equal quality. Of course, they cannot find a substitute model of equal quality because the school team will have identified the best practice.

The third benefit of benchmarking gives the school leader a strategy to accomplish her goals, mission, and vision. The school leader knows specifically what she is doing and why she is doing it, which generates a high level of confidence.

The fourth benefit of benchmarking allows the school leader to demonstrate that the model is working because he has targeted specific measures of performance and outcomes. How often have you heard of schools that implement a program and never measure the program? They never know whether it is successful or unsuccessful. They operate on a qualitative type of feeling. That is not the way quality, high-performance organizations operate.

The fifth benefit of benchmarking is that the program meets the needs of the school community. With their needs met, the members of the school community will give more support and commitment to the school. Each group works to help the other group to meet its needs in a cooperative, collaborative fashion. There is no competition within the school community. Competition focuses outward in the sense that the school team is seeking to develop and employ the benchmarking standard.

The benchmarking process is a natural tool to use in the development and implementation of an effective safe school strategy. In identifying benchmark schools, the effective school leader asks the following questions.[18]

1. Where we will get our benchmark schools?
2. Who identified the school as having the benchmark program?
3. What kinds of standards do we want to have as part of our program?
4. How will we assess the benchmark standards we have adopted?
5. How will we report progress to the community?
6. What are the responsibilities and duties of administrators, teachers, and students?

Answering these questions ensures the school team that they select appropriate benchmarks for emulation.

SUMMARY

This chapter provides the means to identify a vision, mission, SWOT analysis, and benchmarking enabling the school team to develop and implement a safe school plan. These means have widespread applicability to any number of educational and organizational processes. The school leader considers herself as a trainer of trainers. As each of her team members become more skilled in understanding and using these means, they can share this information and skill with other people. For example, the teachers who are members of the school team can teach the SWOT analysis to students to assess their status. How many students fail because they

Putting It Together: Advancing with Vigilance	✓
Did the team develop a vision for the strategic safe school plan? Does everyone understand and embrace the vision? Did the team communicate the vision to the school community? Do the members of the school team understand their mission? Did the team develop a mission and share it with the school community? Has the team identified their point of origin? Has the team identified their destination? Did the team perform a SWOT analysis? Has the team identified the best practices that are currently available? Has the team applied appropriate benchmarks to the strategic safe school plan?	

do not understand their strengths, weaknesses, opportunities, and threats? When teachers can teach students how to organize for success, student-related problems substantially decrease. Students realize that they can control their destiny. Work slowly through each of these means so team members assimilate each action.

NOTES

1. A. Lorri Manasse, "Vision and Leadership: Paying Attention to Intention," *Peabody Journal of Education* 63, no. 1 (1986): 150–73.

2. Thomas Peters, *Thriving on Chaos: Handbook for a Management Revolution* (New York: Harper & Row, 1987), 486–90.

3. Southwest Educational Development Laboratory, "Vision, Leadership, and Change," *Issues about Change* 2, no. 3 (1993), <http://www.sedl.org/change/issues/issues23.html> (2 March 1999).

4. North Central Regional Educational Laboratory, "Components of a Vision," Pathways, http://www.ncrel.org/sdrs/areas/issues/educatrs/leadrshp/le1comps.htm (27 March 2000).

5. Ed Oakley and Doug Krug, *Enlightened Leadership* (New York: Simon & Schuster, 1993), 173.

6. Burt Nanus, *Visionary Leadership: Creating a Compelling Sense of Direction for Your Organization* (San Francisco: Jossey-Bass, 1992), 8.

7. Peter Senge, *The Fifth Discipline* (New York: Doubleday, 1990), <http://learning.mit.edu/res/kr/learningorg.html> (27 March 2000).

8. Warren Bennis and Burt Nanus, *Leaders: Strategies for Taking Charge* (New York: Harper & Row, 1985), 89.

9. "Vision, Values, Purpose, Goals," excerpted from Peter Senge, Art Kleiner, Charlotte Roberts, Richard Ross, and Bryan Smith, *The Fifth Discipline Fieldbook* (1994), <http://learning.mit.edu/pra/lex/vision.html> (27 March 2000).

10. James R. Barker, "Communal-Rational Authority, Control, and Self-managing Teams: Implications for Leadership," Society for Organizational Learning (1999), <http://learning.mit.edu/res/kr/barker/barker-comm.html> (27 March 2000).

11. John Gardner, *Recovery of Confidence* (New York: Norton, 1970), 117.

12. Jocelyn A. Butler, "Clear, Consistent Discipline: Centennial High School," *School Improvement Research Series (SIRS): Snapshot #6,* Northwest Regional Educational Laboratory (February 1988), <http://www.nwrel.org/scpd/sirs/2/snap6.html> (28 March 2000).

13. Kathleen Cotton, "Schoolwide and Classroom Discipline," *School Improvement Research Series (SIRS): Close-Up #9,* Northwest Regional Educational Laboratory (1990), <http://www.nwrel.org/scpd/sirs/5/cu9.html> (28 June 2000).

14. PDK Commission on Discipline, *Directory of Schools Reported to Have Exemplary Discipline* (Bloomington, Ind.: Phi Delta Kappa, 1982), 8 (see Greenfield Junior High School).

15. Elissa Harvey, "Lessons in Violence: A Timeline of Recent School Shootings," *Family Education Network, Infoplease.com* (2000), <http://www.infoplease.com/spot/schoolviolence1.html> (28 March 2000); "Violence at Local Schools," *Palm Beach Post* (28 May 2000), 1A.

16. William H. Wiersema, "What Is Meant by Benchmarking?" *Electrical Apparatus* 51, no. 11 (1998): 43.

17. "Trends Impacting Northwest Education," *Annual Report*, Northwest Regional Education Laboratory (1998), <http://www.nwrel.org/comm/1997ar/3.html> (27 March 2000)

18. This set of six questions was adapted from Robert J. Marzano, "Eight Questions You Should Ask before Implementing Standards-Based Education at the Local Level," *Standards at McRel* (1997), <http://www.mcrel.org/standards/articles/8-questions.asp> (28 March 2000).

CHAPTER SIX

Gaining Agreement

This chapter provides the strategies and tactics to gain agreement on the safe school plan. Gaining agreement encourages the building of solidarity and the development of a sense of community. Gaining agreement is a consensual activity that collectively and collaboratively defines the current school environment. Agreement on a common starting point provides the basis for consensus. In effect, consensus has its genesis in a growing sense of community. This chapter provides a process for the school leader to align perceptions of reality, develop a sense of community, and connect people to a common cause.

In this chapter, you will

- identify the precise conditions of the current environment,
- collect and analyze pertinent data related to the current environment,
- establish conditions that nurture the growth of solidarity among school community members, and
- provide leadership for the implementation of the effective strategy.

CONSENSUS

Consensus is vital to commitment, political support, and community building. M. Scott Peck, noted author on community building, states, "Decisions in genuine community are arrived at through consensus, in a process that is not unlike a community of jurors for whom consensual decision making is mandated."[1] Consensus building is a crucial skill for school leaders. The changing paradigm of school leadership is no longer a hierarchical, authoritarian model but one that is democratic, inclusive, collaborative, and consensual. School leaders who operate out of the old paradigm often have technically sound proposals but discover that their efforts meet growing opposition of those seeking investment in the decision-making process.

Peter Senge, MIT management professor, states, "Pure fads are characterized by a rapid decline, and a complete collapse in interest as the fad fades into obscurity. Ideas of the 1980s have one thing in common—once they're gone, they're gone."[2] This is the critical reason that school leaders need to achieve consensus. Consensus among members of the school community is possible when there is a sense of community. In a consensual community, the members of school community commit themselves to creating a safe and nurturing school environment.

The Importance of Gaining Agreement

As the school leader, you and your team are well into the process of the development and implementation of a safe school plan. The school leader and team members know much about their school and each other. Each step in the process outlined in this book purposely leads to the building of community. The process is beneficial, yet it is when the school community agrees to a starting point that they determine what will exist in the future in terms of performance outcomes. Naming a starting point allows the school leader and her team members to establish a baseline for the development of specific strategies.

School leaders often, because of time deadlines, seek soft levels of agreement. Soft levels of agreement occur when agreement takes precedence to confronting difficult issues and choices. Members give priority to other issues, both personal and professional, rather than to the immediate task. As a result, the desired end is agreement rather than a strategy that addresses specific problems. This soft agreement is efficient but not effective. It selects the first viable solution without considering all possible alternatives.

Irving Janis and Leon Mann, in their seminal work *Decision Making,* write, "The decision maker satisfices rather than maximizes; that is, he looks for a course of action that is good enough, that meets a minimal set of requirements without bothering to compare it with all the alternatives open to them."[3] A "satisficing" strategy (satisfy + suffice) saves time but in the end seldom produces the most effective results. On the other hand, an effective agreement has specific characteristics:

- There is clear understanding and agreement on the available data.
- Commitment is made to others in the process.

- It convey a willingness to suspend personal judgment.
- A desire to arrive at mutually beneficial solutions is expressed.
- There is a commitment to pursue a maximizing decision-making strategy.

Arriving at effective agreements has a greater time cost than do soft agreements. The benefits from effective agreements, however, produce bonds of solidarity and personal commitment that insure that the agreement works. Moving away from a soft agreement approach toward an effective agreement approach requires tenacity, trust, and commitment.

Differing Interpretations of Current Reality

Defining a starting point is a stumbling block for many groups because each team member has a different perception of the starting point. In *The Intelligent Eye,* Richard Gregory states, "We not only believe what we see, to some extent, we see what we believe."[4] What each person sees is a result of his mental conditioning. Take a moment and read Figure 6.1.

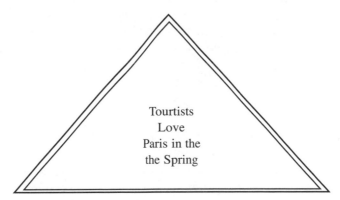

Tourtists
Love
Paris in the
the Spring

Figure 6.1   Differing Interpretations of Reality

This example shows how easy it is to misinterpret reality. Most people will read "Tourists love Paris in the spring." Look again! Read each word slowly. Many people fail to see the second *the*. It actually reads, "Tourists love Paris in the *the* spring." How can two people looking at the same picture see it differently? People have different ways of seeing and of collecting data from the environment. How each person collects data from the environment is unique. The difference in perception leads to disagreements and often conflict. This is one reason that mediation is essential between two disagreeing parties.

According to the Institute for Dispute Resolution:

> A mediator has no power to impose a solution on the parties. Rather, mediators assist parties in shaping solutions to meet their interests and objectives. The mediator's role and the mediation process can take various forms, depending on the nature of the dispute and the approach of the mediator. The mediator can assist parties to communicate effectively; identify and narrow issues; crystallize each side's underlying interests and concerns; carry messages between the parties; explore bases for agreement and the consequences of not settling; and develop a cooperative, problem-solving approach.[5]

Mediation is a necessary skill for the school leader. When the school leader acts as mediator, he assists both sides in discovering common ground. The focused school leader reflects on shared values, the team's metaphor, and guides opposing sides toward a solution.

Resolving disputes is an essential task of the leader. Misperceptions, misrepresentations, and disagreements are the "stuff" of organizational life. For example, two teachers have the same student, yet each teacher has a different perception of that student. One teacher sees the student as a low achiever. Another teacher sees the same student as industrious and a hard worker filled with potential. Where is the true image of this student? Both teachers identify this student based on their image of the student. The student's behavior, relationship with the teacher, the teacher's ideal of a good student, and the teacher's life experiences all influence this image. When the school leader asks each teacher about the student, he will feel as if he is learning about two different students.

The notion of different people having different perceptions extends to all facets of life. Researchers know that when a crime is committed, eyewitnesses give different accounts of the criminal. "The train of thought engaged in by a person trying to make up his or her mind is dominated by the constraints and opportunities, values and norms, that characterizes those interwoven contexts."[6] One wonders who really is the criminal. Women tend to notice more detail than men do as witnesses to a criminal event. Some researchers say we see exactly what we want to see. Even something that others describe as "plain as the nose on your face" is frequently hidden from view. The interpretation and misinterpretation of objective data is a dilemma faced by everyone.

Moving away from multiple interpretations is an essential step in achieving agreement. This process is difficult for team members when others question their view of reality. If the leader, however, assures members that learning to see the whole picture means listening to all perspectives, team members become more open to differing perspectives. The first step in broadening this perspective is to identify objective facts accurately.

The Most Effective Way to Gain Agreement: Gathering Objective Data

Facts are unbiased. They just exist. If we look at enough facts, we come to common agreement about what those facts mean. Hence, one of the most important tasks that the members of the team and the school leader can do to collect the right kinds of facts. The school leader can guide the team to agreement on the depth and breadth of the starting point thorough review of available data. When the school leader presents the objective data, team members avoid disagreements and instead focus on information. The more the school leader guides the team in focusing on the facts, the more successful the team is in gaining widespread agreement on the identification of the starting point for the safe school plan.

Collecting Appropriate Data

The human mind can only handle limited amounts of information in its active state. The human mind is like a computer; after it handles so much information in its RAM, it must store additional information onto its hard disc. If we feed too much information into the RAM, the computer program malfunctions. The human mind also suffers from too much information. Decision researchers state, "Decision makers have information process systems with limited capacities, they must be selective in what they attend to, that is, they can only attend to a subset of the available information in their environment."[7] Too much information provides team members with a sense of accomplishment, but when it comes to examining the data, the team is unable to make appropriate conclusions. If the team collects too little data, the team has a limited sense of reality. The school leader assists the team in finding the appropriate balance by focusing on essential data. One way to achieve this balance is to apply the following heuristic: Act only on a need-to-know basis. Application of this heuristic enables the school leader and her team to work more effectively and efficiently.

The school leader collects data from six areas using qualitative and quantitative skills:

1. Employee background checks
2. Patterns of teacher discipline referrals
3. The community culture
4. Administrative and teacher response to problems and potential problems
5. Symptoms of disorder, potential violence, and related issues
6. Crises preparation

A full examination of the salient data in these six areas leads to the determination of starting point. The goal of collecting data is to identify the starting point. An agreed-to starting point allows members of the school community to work together to resolve mutually identified problems. For example, at Casey-Johnson High School, a major issue for teachers was the number of students cutting class. Administrators felt frustrated in resolving this issue. The school leader and her team collected data for one week related to class cutting. The data revealed the following:

- Less than 1 percent of the student population was cutting class.
- Cutting class occurred 90 percent of the time after lunch.
- Teachers reported student class attendance 85 percent of the time at the end of the day.

As a result, teachers and administrators worked together to develop effective strategies to eliminate class cutting. Rather than provoking confrontation, the data provided an opportunity for collaboration. When the school leader collects appropriate and accurate data, the school team can target the critical sources of safe school problems.

APPLYING APPROPRIATE APPROACHES

The school team can use a series of tools to collect the right data, including the interview design process, needs assessments, database records, and identification of essential groups.

The Interview Design Process

The interview design process[8] allows the school leader to work with groups of school and community members. It generates data on critical questions and increases the quantity and quality of community involvement. The interview design process provides the following benefits:

- It requires the active involvement of all participants.
- It gives equal rank to all opinions.
- It encourages openness and honesty in responding.
- It builds a sense of community by fostering the sharing of stories and experiences.
- It encourages objectivity since the only follow-up questions asked are for clarification.
- It encourages the discovery of common ground through group participation in the analysis of the data that are collected.
- It serves as a motivational tool for participants.

The interview design process takes one to two hours. The school leader and her team prepare for the process by developing interview questions. The school leader divides participants into groups. Each group's membership is equal to the number of the questions used in the process. For example, if there are four critical questions to answer, each small group will have four participants. Each participant has a specific question to ask. To maximize participation, participants act as interviewers and as interviewees. Each interviewer records responses on a data sheet. For example, one question might be "What would you do to improve student behavior at our school?" The respondent states, "Discipline needs to be strict. Teachers can't let students swear in class." The interviewer would record the response. Every five minutes, the respondent and the interviewer change roles and respond to the same question. After both participants fully answer one question, the participants then answer the second question. When both answer and record this question, the moving set of members changes seats and repeat the process. When participants complete the question-and-answer process, they return to their original partners and analyze the data. They look for general themes. The larger group, composed of all smaller groups, discusses the general themes and agrees on a set of themes that embrace all groups.

Needs Assessment

A needs assessment is a commonly used tool in school environments. An effective needs assessment takes planning and an understanding of missing gaps in available information. The application of a few simple guidelines increases the probability that the needs assessment will generate useful data.

An effective needs assessment has several requirements:

1. Each assessment has at least three items worded in a negative pattern.
2. Score each statement on a five-point Likert scale.
3. Target the appropriate population to increase the likelihood of receiving accurate and appropriate data.
4. Develop the needs assessment with sensitivity toward the various cultures in the community.

Each Assessment Has at Least Three Items Worded in a Negative Pattern

A needs assessment sent to parents regarding the discipline at school uses positively and negatively worded statements. A negatively worded statement is "Students at Jones High School are unruly." A positively worded statement is "Students at Jones High School are well behaved." Using randomly placed negatively worded statements in the needs assessment focuses the reader on the questions asked, rather than assuming a certain type of response.

Score Each Statement on a Five-Point Likert Scale

The respondents may answer strongly disagree, disagree, remain undecided, agree, or strongly agree. Depending on the educational level of community, substitute symbols for words. For example, the symbol of a ☺ can mean strongly agree. You must communicate effectively with your community to collect the right kinds of data.

The Likert scale provides five categories. Interpret the undecided category as a negative statement. Often, people who do not agree with the premise of the question will check the undecided mark. They do not support the school administration or teachers on the question; however, they fear identifying themselves as opponents, so they mark undecided. The undecided column infers a lack of support.

Target the Appropriate Population to Increase the Likelihood of Receiving Accurate and Appropriate Data

The third guideline relates to who should receive the needs assessment. For example, sending out five thousand needs assessments to blanket the community is not as effective as identifying a sample of the people from whom you need to collect information. For example, target the needs assessment to a random sample of parents who represent all demographic aspects of the school community. Needs assessments take into account the return rate. As a result, the school leader has mechanisms in place for follow-up and personal collection of data. As a last resort, the school leader and team administer the needs assessment by telephone or home visit.

Develop the Needs Assessment with Sensitivity toward the Various Cultures in the Community

The fourth guideline focuses on cultural sensitivity. If there is a Latino population, the school leader writes the needs assessment in English and Spanish. A person with bilingual skills makes contact and administers the assessment. Many cultures respond more readily when contacted in person rather than through an impersonal letter. The contents and phrasing of the needs assessment also must be considerate of the culture receiving the needs assessment. Phrases that are appropriate in one culture can be insulting to another culture.

Database Records

Another important tool leading to agreement building is the identification and use of information located on the school or school district database. The effective school leader checks to determine the type and extent of available data. Creative analysis processes assess a variety of correlations and levels of significance. In this way, the school leader and team members identify potential at-risk students. Accurate and appropriate data allows the school leader to create targets for strategic action.

Identification of Essential Groups

Identification of essential groups enables the school leader to identify groups that contribute to the development and implementation of a safe school plan. The different community groups exist for a specific purpose, and each group has a coalition network. These coalition networks overlap.

In small communities, members of one group are often members of other groups. In larger communities, connections associate with mutual interests. In either case, community groups have a wide range of interactive relationships. The relationship formed among these groups influences the school community.

Many groups are essential to the development and implementation of an effective strategy. The groups fit one or more of the following categories: community political leaders, juvenile justice professionals, social service agencies, and community-based clergy.

Community Political Leaders

The school leader and her team identify the political leaders in the school and community (see Table 6.1). Political leaders are those in elected or appointed positions or influential members of the school or community who command respect and help to shape policy. Political leaders comprise current and former office holders within the school's community, including former political leaders such as those who served as mayor, school board members, and city counsel members.

Political leaders also act in informal leadership roles. They are the people behind the formal leaders. These people respond favorably to informal meetings such as lunches or interviews.

The effective school leader, when consulting political leaders, makes sure to consult all the political leaders within his school and community. He knows that there is a risk of creating adversaries if he ignores any political leader.

Juvenile Justice Professionals

Juvenile justice professionals are probation officers, juvenile judges, and police officers who work with students involved in criminal or the prevention of criminal activity. Often, students who are in trouble with the

Table 6.1 Community Political Leaders

Group	Contact Person	Position	Phone Number	Priority
Band Boosters Club	Marsha Stalz	President	555-1234	3
PTA	John Crandel	President	555-4321	2
Athletic Support Team	Terry Simpson	Chairperson	555-6789	4
City Council	Larry Johnson	Mayor	555-0987	1
MADD	Lillie Toggert	Chairperson	555-8989	5
Chamber of Commerce	Gilbert Garza	Executive director	555-3232	6

law are in trouble within the school system. Juvenile justice professionals have insights into problems that school administrators encounter each day. For example, the school team may not be aware of an adolescent drug problem because there is no visible evidence of drugs in the school. The members of the juvenile justice system, however, may report that they have had many arrests of students using a variety of drugs. They may have evidence that a hidden drug problem exists.

The Internet also has significant information related to juvenile justice. For example, Curtis High School has a gang handbook available on-line that provides detailed information about school gangs and related research. You can access this information at http://www.upsd.wednet.edu/UPSD/CHS/ganghand.html. This information provides valuable data pertaining to gangs and strategies found effective in dealing with gangs.

Social Service Agencies

Social service agencies are in constant contact with parents and their children. They are aware of issues related to the families in the school district. A social worker provides information not readily available to school officials. For example, a student may be consistently late to school. This student may not want to share her reasons for tardiness. The social worker may have background data regarding a student's tardiness to school. The social worker knows that the student is late because the only adult in the home leaves at 5:00 A.M. for work; the student has to remain at home until the younger children go to school. The social worker may also be aware of instances of sexual or physical abuse, drug abuse, or unemployment.

Community-Based Clergy

In many areas, clergy play an important community role. In some regions, the community church is the base for social and political action. In the Midwest or Southwest, the school leader may find more than 90 percent of a community belonging to a single church within the community. The pastor of the church, in these communities, is influential. In other, urban areas, the school's location may serve a demographic population representing one dominant faith group. It is important to contact the clergy to discover the concerns of the members of their church.

The clergy and the members of his church want to be supporters of school efforts. Clergy members have political and grassroots connections. Gaining their support for initiatives begins by involving them in the process.

ANALYZING DATA

The school leader guides the team in analyzing data before drawing conclusions. Each team member shares the data she collected with the entire team. This is not a rushed process. In one meeting, members focus on quantitative data. In another meeting, members analyze qualitative data. The analysis creates baseline data. Baseline data assists the school leader in establishing agreement as to the depth and breadth of the issues.

The school leader encourages the team to resist the temptation to draw conclusions. Instead, the school leader focuses on objectively analyzing the data. The school leader and team examine the analyzed data looking for trends and patterns. The effective school leader knows that all data present patterns, albeit often obscure ones. They exist, however, in behavior among students, teachers, administrators, and parents. These patterns indicate where baseline problems exist. If the problems exist with people, then the team can target knowledge and skill acquisition. If the problems exist because of policy, then the school leader and team can target policy revision.

REPORT FINDINGS TO THE COMMUNITY

The school leader and her team need to develop an objective report clearly identifying trends and patterns supported by existing data. This report is "accurate and useful. [It] enables teachers, students, parents and the public to understand why various instruments are being applied and how the results will be used as part of the school improvement process."[9] The attachment of data demonstrates the thoroughness of the school leader's investigation. The report explains what the data show to exist, which allows people to accept the report and work together toward common solutions.

The school leader shares the report with appropriate groups. The Michigan State Board of Education has the following recommendations: "It is necessary to identify: Who needs or wants the information you have, what information should be reported, why the reporting is being done—the expected outcome of the reporting, and how the formation can best be transmitted to reach the intended audience(s)."[10] Since the school leader should use this report to develop grassroots support for her safe school plan, she realizes that viable parties include the superintendent, appropriate central office personnel, school board members, teachers, parents, students, and other community members. Her goal in sharing this report is to gain community support. This report generates critical grassroots support.

A CONSENSUS MODEL

Consensus is a time-consuming growth process that allows a synergy of multiple ideas to occur. A number of consensus-building models are available. Each of these models can lead a team that has a consensus-generating environment toward consensus.

One model, developed by Quest, is Snowflake. This model encourages full participation throughout the consensus-driven process. Quest describes the model in detail on-line at http://www.ael.org/rel/quest/snowfl.htm. A second model described by Mary Randall suggests ways for building consensus among teacher teams. This model provides all participants the chance to influence the group's ultimate decision. Commitment to the outcome and long-term support for the ultimate decision are central to this process. The process is available on-line at http://NCRVE.BERKELEY.EDU/CW63/BuildingConsensus.html. In the end, all consensus models seem to have the central values of openness, full participation, and commitment to a final product.

The following components are essential to the consensus process. The effective school leader uses these components to build a consensus environment in her team and school community. It is in this environment that the school leader creates sustained support for the safe school plan.

- The school leader creates solidarity.
- The school leader links consensus to understanding the multifaceted nature of the members of the school community.
- The school leader clarifies perceptions among team members and members of the school community.
- The school leader encourages each team member to identify personal views of a safe school.
- The school leader identifies points of reconciliation.
- The school leader identifies points of contention.

Creating Solidarity

Creating solidarity among group members develops consensus. The school leader builds solidarity by creating a trusting environment. The school leader creates an environment where solidarity and community are at the core. Solidarity moves beyond collegial relationships. It means that each member of the organization cares about the rights and welfare of all others in the organization. These actions, when universal within the organization, synergistically transform the environment and generate widespread trust. When people recognize that trust exists, they move from confrontation to consensus.

The effective school leader applies six critical factors to create solidarity among the members of her school:

1. Willingness to trust the experience of others
2. Willingness to listen to members of the school and community
3. Willingness to lower personal defenses
4. Willingness to ask questions to gain clarification
5. Willingness to take personal responsibility for making the relationship work
6. Willingness to act to heal conflict

Willingness to Trust the Experience of Others

School leaders build solidarity through trust. Respecting other people and their experiences develops trust. When the school leader and her team trust each other's set of experiences, they validate each other's experience. Each person's unique experience allows us to understand the context in which we are collectively involved. By trusting other people's experience, we build solidarity.

For example, Roosevelt High School is in a demographic area that has a high percentage of people on welfare. The community supports the school because they feel the faculty and administration understand community issues. These members of the community surrounding Roosevelt High School do not feel shamed or condemned based on their socioeconomic status. The administration and faculty of Roosevelt High School discovered that when community members have their experiences validated, the community members willingly participate in creating an effective school.

Willingness to Listen to Members of the School and Community

Effective school leaders listen to members of the school and community. They use effective communication skills to build solidarity. The key to effective communication is *active listening*. The kinds of listening skills that build solidarity are those that process and understand what the other person is saying. When the school leader listens for understanding, she understands the message without judging the person speaking. In seeking to understand the message, the school leader seeks to understand the motivation behind the message.

Clive Adams, principal at Big Mountain Middle School, had a success-ful experience in building solidarity with a parent of a student he sus-pended. At first, the parent was against out-of-school suspension. In Clive's discussions with the parent, he recognized the parent's anger to the out-of-school suspension. In seeking to understand the parent's motiva-tion, Clive discovered that this was a single parent. The parent worked during the day, and out-of-school suspension meant that the student would not have direct supervision during the day. This parent did not oppose out-of-school suspension. The parent opposed having his child unsupervised during the day. Clive and the parent worked together to build a mutually satisfactory agreement. In this way, school leaders, like Clive, demon-strate that understanding the motivations of people builds solidarity and solves problems.

Willingness to Lower Personal Defenses

The effective school leader works to lower personal defenses. Solidar-ity eliminates defensive reactions to those who have different perspec-tives. Defensiveness often leads to a series of counterattacks. The result is an unnecessary confrontation with a critical person or group. These confrontations hamper the ultimate success of the safe school plan. Rather than creating a cycle of conflict through a defensive reaction, the school leader reserves the moral high ground and often gains sup-port of the community.

Willingness to Ask Questions to Gain Clarification

The effective school leader asks questions to gain clarification. Questions are necessary to the growth process. The use of questions focuses atten-tion on potential outcomes. When the school leader asks the right ques-tion, he increases his opportunities to find the right solution. If he asks the wrong question, he may find the right answer to the wrong question, but the problem remains.

The effective school leader recognizes the difference between questions that gain clarification and questions interpreted as probing. A probing question causes defensiveness. Examples of probing questions are "Why did you do that? What were the reasons you did that? What did you expect to gain from that?" Questions that seek to gain clarification are "How has this experience affected you? In what ways can this experience help other people? Can you tell me more about that situation?" The use of probing questions promotes defensiveness. Clarifying questions help validate experience. When questions seek to clarify meaning, they construct an environment where willingness to share replaces defensive reactions.

Willingness to Take Personal Responsibility for Making the Relationship Work

The effective school leader takes personal responsibility for making the relationship work. In every successful relationship, at least one party takes responsibility to make it work. The relationship, however, is more effective when both parties take responsibility. Effective school leaders initiate that responsibility. They take responsibility for making a relationship work by acting inclusively toward others, validating experience, and showing sincere interest in the person.

Mary Hillman, principal of Labett Elementary School, gives others her full attention. When a person is sitting in her office and the phone rings, Mary refuses to divert her attention to the phone call. Her actions let her visitor know that that the phone call is not as important as the conversation. She knows that each time she ignores the phone or beeper and focuses her attention on the other person, she demonstrates a willingness to build a relationship and enter into solidarity.

Willingness to Act to Heal Conflict

The effective school leader acts to heal conflict. She recognizes that conflict is a natural part of life and inevitable. The school leader, however, understands that conflict is often the way that people negotiate their paths through difficult problems. The effects of conflict are often psychologically painful, and they can negatively affect the group by destroying future attempts at consensus.

The school leader can heal the painful remnants of conflicts through reconciliation. Effective school leaders are primarily reconcilers. They constantly reconcile differences among members of their organization. The school leader takes responsibility for reconciliation. Martin Luther King Jr. described the process of reconciliation as not forgetting one's experience but not allowing one's experience to influence the present moment. King, in his "I Have a Dream" speech, spoke about the critical nature of reconciliation as being basic to any foundation of solidarity and community when he stated:

> But there is something that I must say to my people who stand on the warm threshold which leads into the palace of justice. In the process of gaining

our rightful place, we must not be guilty of wrongful deeds. Let us not seek to satisfy our thirst for freedom by drinking from the cup of bitterness and hatred. We must forever conduct our struggle on the high plane of dignity and discipline. We must not allow our creative protest to degenerate into physical violence. Again and again we must rise to the majestic heights of meeting physical force with soul force. The marvelous new militancy which has engulfed the Negro community must not lead us to distrust of all white people, for many of our white brothers, as evidenced by their presence here today, have come to realize that their destiny is tied up with our destiny and their freedom is inextricably bound to our freedom. We cannot walk alone.[11]

Failure to reconcile destroys many organizations. Residual anger becomes a part of the school culture that destroys attempts at building solidarity. Someone has to take responsibility to mediate conflict. As successful mediators point out, the underlying problems for most conflicts are rather simple and insignificant. Yet, conflict escalates based on individual bias. It takes the skill of someone who is willing to work with two antagonistic parties to resolve the issues that separate them. This person is the school leader.

Understanding the Multifaceted Nature of the Members of the School Community

Creating a climate where consensus is possible requires the school leader's awareness of the multifaceted nature of the school community. Awareness leads to inclusion. Inclusion leads to community and consensus. It enables the school leader to build solidarity.

Understanding the multifaceted nature of the school community has three components:

1. The identification of personal areas of strength of school community members
2. The identification of personal areas of concern
3. The identification with others' experience

The Identification of Personal Areas of Strength of School Community Members

Creating a climate conducive to building consensus begins through the recognition of the strengths that each person brings to the school community. Joe Batten, management consultant, suggests that the new wave of leadership focus on the strengths of its members. He recommends that leaders learn how to conduct a strengths analysis of members.[12] The results of the strengths analysis provide the leader with an effective way to group and use each person's strengths.

A strengths analysis is a way to generate mutual acknowledgment of member strengths. When adversaries acknowledge each other's strengths, mutual respect is the result.

The process of conducting a strengths analysis is straightforward. If the school leader conducts the strength analysis with her team, she has each member list four personal strengths on paper. Once each person lists their four strengths, they share these strengths with the team. The team discovers a collective list of strengths. This process builds personal and team self-esteem. As each member shares his or her strengths, a sense of mutual respect develops.

The Identification of Personal Areas of Concern

The effective school leader identifies areas related to the issue that are of concern to any member of the team. Once the school leader identifies all areas of concern, he refers to the strengths analysis and tags each concern with a strength identified in the strength analysis. By tagging concerns with strengths, the school leader and his team recognize that they have the resources to overcome the challenges presented by these concerns. For example, a team member may express concern that he does not understand the problems of single parents in raising children. One of the strengths of a team member may be that of a single parent who has successfully raised two children. Her strength addresses the concerns of this person.

The willingness to identify concerns and link concerns to strengths creates a sense of confidence in the group and facilitates the building of consensus.

The Identification with the Others' Experience

The school leader encourages each member to share personal experiences related to raising or educating their children. Each time a member speaks about her fears, frustrations, and hopes, other members discover the depth of human similarities. Team members discover that their dreams, joys, and painful experiences are similar. This process creates a climate of psychological identification. In my work with widely diverse teams, I discovered that this single process of self-explanation is a decisive factor in building solidarity.

Clarifying Perceptions

The effective school leader clarifies perceptions. She recognizes that each person has a different perspective. The school leader assumes the responsibility to understand these multiple perspectives and to lead team members to common ground. Once the leader understands the diverse viewpoints, she can facilitate the consensus process. She knows that framing is critical to this procedure. A *frame* is a reference point for a behavioral response. To achieve consensus, the school leader references the frame of members toward conciliation and integration.

Effective leaders see the whole process in a Hegelian framework of thesis, antithesis, and synthesis. Each person's reference point is a starting point for discussion. As each person clarifies his or her ideas within the context of a team, the process of synthesis begins. The synthesis is not so much one of compromise; rather, it is a moving toward a synergy of opposing views. The synergy of opposing views is a new view that emerges from the seeds of the original conceptions of the differing parties. This synergy emerges when members are willing to be open to new possibilities. The way to be open to new possibilities is to release the original reference point.

One way the school leader helps team members to understand this process is to have team members share memories of an important material possession that they had when they were younger. After each team member shares his or her feelings about this important object, ask them how important that object is now. The answer is obvious: it is no longer important. The member discarded it many years ago. The member's reference point to the object changed. It is the same way with current reference points. A year from now a once critical reference point will not be important. In that light, a reference point becomes a point from which we want to grow and to enable others to grow. Clarification leads to the gaining of perspective and the gaining of perspective leads to consensus.

Identifying Personal Views of Safe Schools

The effective school leader asks team members to identify personal beliefs about the construction of a safe school. This process focuses on the relationship factors inherent in developing an effective safe school strategy. Hidden in these perceptions regarding safe schools are each team member's underlying values. These underlying values drive behavior. A technically sound strategic safe school initiative surrounded by destructive attitudes undermines any chance for success.

Dialogue among members in a safe environment helps to construct and reconstruct personal beliefs regarding students, teachers, parents, teaching, and discipline.

> While dialogue brings critical issues into open debate, [it is] principally concerned with human relationships. Organized dialogue operates on the assumption that all people have pre-existing relationships—no matter whether adversarial, friendly, or tenuous—which must be overcome. Passive and unequal relationships are overcome by building active relationships. The very difficult task of working across boundaries of social roles, wealth, ethnicity, race, gender, and occupation is facilitated by dialogues' focus on issues, no matter how contentious. Dialogues ideally bring together people with diverse opinions who are willing to seriously and respectfully discuss an issue.[13]

Through the constructive use of dialogue, the school leader guides team members in the discovery of each other's point of view regarding the safe school plan. This process creates an open environment minimizing hidden agendas.

Identifying Points of Reconciliation

The effective school leader identifies points of reconciliation. He knows that reconciliation of differences begins by identifying points of similarity that lead to the discovery of common ground. He assists the team in discovering common ground by framing the process into one of cooperation rather than confrontation.

The school leader uses a large circle, a symbol of solidarity, listing all points of similarity to stimulate the process of reconciliation of differences. This type of symbolism demonstrates how differing views can coexist and support each other. Roger Fisher and William Ury from the Harvard Negotiations Project state, "The principle negotiation method of focusing on basic interests, mutually satisfying options, and fair standards typically result in a wise agreement permitting you to reach a gradual consensus on a joint decision efficiently without all the transactional costs of digging in to positions only to have to dig yourself out of them."[14]

Identifying Points of Contention

The effective school leader resolves points of contention not allowing them to undermine team solidarity. For example, one member does not believe in out-of-school suspension of students. Another member believes that violent students and students selling drugs should be suspended. The school leader resolves points of contention by encouraging members to state their positions by identifying desired outcomes. Once they state their desired outcomes, they suggest an alternative, which results in the relaxation of rigidly held positions. By reframing the focus to inquire into outcomes, members discover common ground. In the disagreement regarding suspension of students, both parties can agree on the safety of school members. They can agree on a punishment for those who commit violence toward others and the need to make this issue a learning experience. This opens a new paradigm because members can ask "What other model besides the one suggested by both parties can we use that will meet these particular needs?" In this way, opposing parties become collaborators in seeking a solution. They change contention into collaboration. When this happens, solidarity occurs and members achieve consensus. Any time a team moves through conflict into a collaborative process, they meet success by overcoming obstacles to growth.

SUMMARY

This chapter teaches school community members how to gain agreement, build solidarity, and achieve consensus on the safe school plan. The effective school leader recognizes that the school team needs to gain agreement on problems. She knows that the path to gaining agreement lies in helping team members begin by discovering a common starting point. This chapter focuses on the importance of using data as a means for discovering this common starting point. With proper information, the school leader facilitates the overcoming of barriers.

The use of the right kind of data allows the team to gain an understanding of the problems faced by the school. In gaining this type of data, members need to apply relationship-building skills within the team and in the greater school community. Six critical factors facilitate the building of solidarity among team members. These factors enable the school team to build solidarity within the team and to go out beyond the confines of the team to build solidarity with other members of the school community. By moving out of the team into the community, the team and the community make a commitment to a common cause.

This chapter also addresses how the school team can gain agreement on an array of issues. This process moves the team members from contention to collaboration, conflict to reconciliation, and accusation to understanding.

Putting It Together: Advancing with Vigilance	✓
Did the team collect the "right" data? Did the team analyze the data? Did the team find themes and patterns within the data? Did the team identify a common reality about what is happening? Did the team reconstruct and reframe negative and nonproductive attitudes into constructive and productive attitudes? Did the team make an effort to create solidarity with all groups within the community? Does the team have a sense of solidarity? Did the team make a special effort to reach out to minority parents for input? Did the team reach into the community for input?	

NOTES

1. M. Scott Peck, *The Different Drum* (New York: Simon & Schuster, 1987), 63.

2. Peter Senge, *The Fifth Discipline: The Art and Practice of the Learning Organization* (New York: Doubleday, 1990), x.

3. Irving Janis and Leon Mann, *Decision Making* (New York: Free Press, 1977), 25.

4. Richard Gregory, *The Intelligent Eye* (New York: McGraw-Hill, 1970), 3.

5. "The ABCs of ADR: A Dispute Resolution Glossary," Institute of Dispute Resolution (1995), <http://www.cpradr.org/glossary.htm#mediat> (27 March 2000).

6. Tod S. Soan, *Deciding: Self-deception Life Choices* (New York: Methuen, 1987), 1.

7. R. Phelps, R. Pliske, and S. Mutter, "Improving Decision Making: A Cognitive Approach," in *Human Productivity Enhancement*, ed. Joseph Zeidner (New York: Praeger, 1987), vol. 2: 303.

8. Oralie McAfee, "The Interview Design Process," Appalachia Regional Educational Laboratory, <http://www.ael.org/rel/quilt/interv.htm> (27 March 2000).

9. Edward D. Roeber, "Critical Issue: Reporting Assessment Results," North Central Regional Educational Laboratory (1995), <http://www.ncrel.org/sdrs/areas/issues/methods/assment/as600.htm> (27 March 2000).

10. Michigan State Board of Education, "Pencils Down," North Central Regional Educational Laboratory (1989), <http://www.ncrel.org/sdrs/areas/issues/methods/assment/as6penc2.htm> (27 March 2000).

11. Martin Luther King Jr., "I Have a Dream," Washington, D.C., 18 August 1963, <http://web66.coled.umn.edu/new/MLK/MLK.html> (27 March 2000).

12. Joseph Batten, *Tough Minded Leadership* (New York: AMACOM, 1989).

13. Brett Lane and Diane Dorfman, "Strengthening Community Networks: The Basis for Sustainable Community Renewal," Northwest Regional Educational Laboratory (1997), <http://www.nwrel.org/ruraled/Strengthening.html> (27 March 2000).

14. Roger Fisher and William Ury, *Getting to Yes* (New York: Penguin, 1981), 14.

CHAPTER SEVEN

The Knowledge Base

This chapter requires the school leader to take an action orientation and results focus. The leader and his team move from conceptual planning to the application, adaptation, and invention of strategies and tactics grounded in a knowledge base and expressed through long and short-range objectives. The knowledge base provides insights into effective safe school strategies. In effect, the school leader and his team use their knowledge base to develop effective strategies, understand the essential issue of linking timing to strategies, and focus on attaining long- and short-term objectives.

In this chapter, you will

- identify nationally recognized safe school strategies,
- identify a knowledge base related to effective safe schools,
- apply the principles in Maslow's hierarchy of needs,
- focus on attaining long- and short-term objectives,
- apply the window concept, and
- apply the medical model to short-range strategies.

The school leader who accurately and appropriately identifies short- and long-term objectives produces immediate success and sustains school and community support. By achieving short- and long-term objectives, the school leader demonstrates high levels of competence and engenders community-wide confidence in the safe school plan. For example, consider the actions of Long Beach, California, school leaders:

In 1994, the Long Beach California School District implemented a mandatory school uniform policy for nearly 60,000 elementary and middle school students. District officials found that in the year following implementation of the policy, overall crime decreased 36 percent, fights decreased 51 percent, sex offenses decreased 74 percent, weapons offenses decreased 50 percent, assault and battery offenses decreased 34 percent and vandalism decreased 18 percent.[1]

Planned action builds community confidence in the school leader's ability to effectively lead and manage the school.

THE STRATEGIC KNOWLEDGE BASE

The purpose of this book is to provide a school–community facilitation process that results in the development, implementation, and success of a complex safe school plan. This facilitation process is rich in its ability to build community, generate a sense of common ground, and provide for the collective development of a vision, mission, goals, and clearly stated objectives. The grassroots and consensual nature of this process produces widespread buy-in. At some stage in the strategic development process, however, if the safe school plan is to be ultimately successful, the school leader will have to make decisions based on available information. This information has to be accurate, up-to-date, and applicable to the school leader's context. There is a panoply of accessible information on safe schools, school discipline, and school violence. For example, a recent search of the Office of Juvenile Justice files indicated more than five thousand files related to school discipline.

The amount of data available and the time needed to review this data can overwhelm even the most organized person or team. This chapter provides you with essential data, references, and Internet resources to facilitate your data research and review. Ultimately, the school community determines the safe school plan. Effective safe school plans will differ from one community to the next. Although each school and its surrounding community are different, they share thirteen specific characteristics that allow early detection of potential problems[2] (see Table 7.1). The school leader and her team can apply these characteristics to rate the safe school environment in their school.

These thirteen characteristics focus more on the quality of the school and the education experience than on the specifics of safe school planning. They focus on the importance of creating a school community where everyone sees themselves as a partner in the process of creating a safe school environment. These characteristics focus on the necessity of com-

Table 7.1 Characteristics of a Safe School

Characteristics	Self-Rating Scale (degree to which characteristic is present: 1—nonexistent, to 10—clearly present)
1. Safe schools focus on academic achievement.	1 2 3 4 5 6 7 8 9 10
2. Safe schools include the families of students in important ways.	1 2 3 4 5 6 7 8 9 10
3. Safe schools develop important connections to the community.	1 2 3 4 5 6 7 8 9 10
4. Safe schools stress positive connections among students and adults in the school environment.	1 2 3 4 5 6 7 8 9 10
5. Safe schools openly discuss issues of safety with students, teachers, parents, and community members.	1 2 3 4 5 6 7 8 9 10
6. Safe schools provide environments where all students are treated with equal respect.	1 2 3 4 5 6 7 8 9 10
7. Safe schools provide avenues for students to share their concerns with adults in the school.	1 2 3 4 5 6 7 8 9 10
8. Safe schools encourage and allow students to share their feelings to school personnel.	1 2 3 4 5 6 7 8 9 10
9. Safe schools have a system in place that quickly refers children where there is suspicion of abuse or neglect.	1 2 3 4 5 6 7 8 9 10
10. Safe schools offer extensive extended day programs.	1 2 3 4 5 6 7 8 9 10
11. Safe schools promote exemplary citizenship and character.	1 2 3 4 5 6 7 8 9 10
12. Safe schools recognize problems and evaluate progress toward solutions.	1 2 3 4 5 6 7 8 9 10
13. Safe schools advocate for students who are making the progression from student to adult life and entering the workplace.	1 2 3 4 5 6 7 8 9 10

Source: This table is quoted and adapted to tabular form from *Early Warning, Timely Response: A Guide to Safe Schools,* the referenced edition, Center for Effective Collaboration and Practice (1999), <http://www.air-dc.org/cecp/guide/annotated.htm> (5 April 2000).

munication from teacher to student, student to teacher, school staff to parents, and parents to school staff. In essence, these characteristics sustain a nurturing and compassionate learning environment.

A caring environment is a central component of a safe school plan. In caring schools, teachers use their healthy sense of self-esteem to create a supportive and nurturing environment. This environment "develops and applies rules and offers specialized assistance in ways that recognize that the matter of fairness involves such complicated questions as, Fair for whom? Fair according to whom? Fair using what criteria and what procedures for applying the criteria?"[3] In addition, caring schools create an atmosphere where teachers, students, and visitors feel respected, valued, and at ease. These schools provide an environment where students build and nurture healthy relationships with each other and with the adults in the school. These schools create an environment where students have a clear understanding of expectations and how to meet those standards. The school administrators, teachers, and staff in these schools provide students with guidance, counseling, training, and encouragement to adopt new, more empowering belief systems. Within these successful school environments, school leaders integrate social and emotional functioning issues into the curriculum.

The W. T. Grant Foundation reported the results of a five-year project that synthesized the core social and emotional competencies. Table 7.2 identifies these competencies.[4]

Safe schools with caring and nurturing environments are the result of hard work, planning, and commitment by school administrators, teachers, parents, students, and community members. In these communities, members turn from blaming each other and join to seek collaborative solutions that transform their schools and community. The members of the community realize that each person has a role to play and that no single role is greater than any other role. For example, some suggest that the school leader has the responsibility for developing programs, building grassroots support, monitoring progress, and maintaining an environment that is fair, just, inclusive, and equitable.[5] Effective safe schools clearly define roles. School leaders know that parents are an essential part of this process.

Parental Involvement

Parents play an important role in creating and sustaining a safe school. Parents whose children attend safe schools are proactive in their involvement with their child's school. Their proactive stance makes them part of the school's learning environment. Proactive parents explain rules to their children, teach their children to solve problems, help their children discover new and creative ways to resolve conflict, and guide their children in setting instructional and behavioral priorities. These proactive parents are not strangers to their child's school. They do not have to wait for an invitation to visit the school. Consequently, teachers, counselors, and administrators know these parents. In safe schools, these parents are partners.

According to the *Annual Report on School Safety*, effective schools encourage parents to communicate with their children, be firm in their

Table 7.2 Core Social and Emotional Competencies

Emotional Competencies	Cognitive Competencies	Behavioral Competencies
• Ability to recognize and label feelings	• Uses self-talk to cope with a challenge or reinforce behavior	• Understands how to communicate effectively in non-verbal ways. For example, applies eye contact, facial indications, speech, and gestures
• Ability to express personal feelings	• Understands how to fit into the larger community	• Understands how to communicate effectively in verbal ways. For example, the student knows how to make clear requests, respond effectively to criticism, resists nonaffirming influences, listens to others, and contributes meaningfully and actively in peer discussions
• Ability to estimate the depth of personal feelings • Ability to regulate feelings and emotions • Ability to delay desire to immediate gratification	• Applies an appropriate problem solving and decision making process • Is able to understand the feelings and perspectives of other people • Can distinguish between what is acceptable and what is not acceptable in terms of personal behavior • Develops practical personal expectations • Maintains an optimistic attitude toward life and own future	

Source: This table is quoted and adapted to tabular form from "Curriculum Content for Enhancing Social and Emotional Functioning," *Addressing Barriers to Learning 2*, no. 2 (Spring 1997), School Mental Health Project, UCLA, <http://smhp.psych.ucla.edu/lesson22.htm> (5 April 2000).

discipline practices, model prosocial behavior, become actively involved in school and community activities, keep guns and destructive devices out of the home environment, reduce their child's exposure to crime and violence, and involve the family in family training or counseling possibilities.[6]

In some ways, developing parent–school partnerships is at the core of any emerging safe school. According to Family/School Partnerships, the following guidelines ensure partnership success:[7]

- The school leader and team assess family needs and interests in co-operating with schools.
- The school leader understands that parent input enhances communication and promotes cooperation.
- The school leader employs a trained liaison to work directly with parents.
- The school leader understands the importance of establishing effective relationships with minority parents.
- The school leader gives priority to multimedia ways of communicating with parents.
- Central to investing parents in developing and sustaining a safe school is the ability of teachers to work directly with parents. Teachers and administrators need training in constructing partnerships.

Involving parents in the planning process creates a greater chance for widespread support for plans that result in a safe school. The involvement of parents on a planned, consistent, and meaningful basis builds a climate of trust. A climate of trust among the community, parents, teachers, and administrators creates an ideal climate that nurtures the development of a safe school environment. In this environment, characteristics emerge that mark the school as a safe school (see Table 7.3). Researchers indicate that these characteristics are lacking in poorly disciplined schools.[8]

Safe School Characteristics

Creating a safe school is not an illusion. How is it that some schools create safe havens for learning while other schools struggle year after year? Schools that create safe havens have approaches as distinct as their geographic locations. Researchers can identify eight essential factors that transcend safe schools, regardless of location or context:

1. Safe schools establish behavior criterion.
2. Safe schools provide competent adult nearness, oversight, and connection to and with students.
3. Safe schools enforce discipline judiciously and consistently.

Table 7.3 Safe School Characteristics

Safe School Characteristic	Description of Characteristic
Commitment to establishing and maintaining high standards of student behavior as a prerequisite for learning	• All members of the school community work to achieve the same end. • There is a high level of commitment to achieve goals. • There is a shared belief that high levels of student instructional performance relate directly to maintaining high standards for behavioral performance.
High behavioral expectations	• Expectations are clear. • The school leader communicates expectations to teachers, parents, and students. • Administrators and teachers share a common set of high expectations for personal performance as well as student behavior and performance.
Clear and broad-based rules	• Rules, penalties, and process have broad-based input including that of students. • Rules, penalties, and process are communicated to students, staff, and parents. • Administrators and teachers carefully follow rules, penalties, and process. • There is no ambiguity as to what to expect from the identified rules, penalties, and process.
Warm school climate	• There is a deep concern by administrators and teachers for students as individuals. • Student issues are paramount. • Administrators identify the needs of students. • Teachers relate directly to students. • People care for each other.
Visible, supportive principal	• Principal is visible in the hallways. • Principal is visible in the classrooms. • Principal knows students by name. • Principal expresses interest in students' lives. • Principal is supportive of teacher needs.
Close ties with the community	• Partnerships established with the school community. • Parents are involved in school activities. • Parents and the school community are informed of school issues, goals, and activities. • The school acts inclusively toward members of the community.
Delegation of discipline authority to teachers	• Principals handle serious discipline cases. • Teachers have authority and responsibility to handle routine classroom discipline problems. • Principals work with teachers to improve classroom management skills. • Principals work with teachers to provide for appropriate staff development to improve teacher instructional and behavioral management skills.

Source: This table quoted and adapted to tabular form from Kathleen Cotton, "Schoolwide and Classroom Discipline," *School Improvement Research Series* (SIRS), *Close-Up #9* (December 1990), Northwest Regional Educational Laboratory.

4. Safe schools supervise and consistently correct those students who violate school rules.
5. Safe schools make parents partners in the discipline process.
6. Safe schools make the school building and its environment a safe space.
7. Safe schools form partnerships with external agencies such as juvenile justice officials.
8. Safe schools maintain an underlying belief that the school can make a constructive difference in the lives of the children attending the school.[9]

Implicit in these eight factors are specific themes. Clearly, the notion of caring in the sense of tough love is evident in these factors. The adults in safe schools care enough to be present to young people; they care enough to use the violation of discipline rules as a constructive and learning experience; they care enough to make sure that their actions are fair and just.

A second theme throughout these eight factors is a systemic approach to school discipline. School discipline is the entire community's responsibility. Within this framework is the belief that the environment contributes to a safe school as much as what the teacher does in the classroom.

Ronald Stephens proposed a series of strategies to prevent school violence and increase school safety:[10]

1. Monitor access to the school campus.
2. Develop an excellent extracurricular program.
3. Maintain accurate records.
4. Cooperate with all the appropriate community agencies.
5. Make school safety a priority component of the school's mission statement.
6. Review and revise the student handbook.
7. Clearly define locker policy.
8. Construct a schoolwide strategic discipline plan.
9. Develop and implement a clear student dress code.
10. Advise everyone of legal issues and rights.
11. Prevent weapons on campus.
12. Keep abreast of technological advances related to safe schools.
13. Provide adequate adult supervision.
14. Treat the threat of violence as actual violence.
15. Define parking policies.

16. Implement visitor-screening procedures.
17. Create and practice a crisis response plan.
18. Require school security to undergo training in dealing with adolescents and children.
19. Identify the responsibilities associated with each administration, faculty, and staff member's role related to school discipline.
20. Incorporate decision making, life skills, conflict negotiating into the formal school curriculum.
21. Create alternative settings for students unable to function in the traditional school environment.
22. Involve students in peer counseling and peer mediation.
23. Teacher and staff training needs to be ongoing and up-to-date.
24. Understand each culture represented in the school.
25. Promote a safe school environment through appropriate building and grounds modifications.
26. Create a climate of faculty, parent, and student ownership and pride in their school.
27. Carefully select new faculty and staff.

The school leader asks her team to reflect on these strategies as a means of stimulating creative thinking as they design their safe school plan. She knows that benchmark schools identify a wide range of strategies and adapt them to the needs of their school and community. These school leaders recognize the faulty strategy in the unquestioned application of a successful model from another organization. Nonetheless, they are cognizant that they can learn from the practices of others. In essence, a school becomes a learning organization.

The School as a Learning Organization

Learning organizations have people committed to learning.

[These people] are engaged in their work, striving to reach their potential, by sharing the vision of a worthy goal with team colleagues. They have mental models to guide them in the pursuit of personal mastery, and their personal goals are in alignment with the mission of the organization. Working in a learning organization is seeing one's work as part of a whole, a system where there are interrelationships and processes that depend on each other.[11]

Essentially, members of a learning organization understand knowledge management and knowledge generation.

Schools are essentially learning organizations. When the school leader and his team integrate the existing knowledge base on safe schools, they are acting as a learning organization. The school leader uses knowledge management in three ways:

1. He makes knowledge the foundation for all actions.
2. He uses knowledge to develop creative and sound strategic decisions to meet the needs of the school and community.
3. He applies the best knowledge available to strategic decisions and actions.[12]

When a school becomes a learning organization, it demonstrates that it operates in a continual growth cycle. As change affects the school, the school learns how to adapt to change rather than resist change. Members of learning organizations know where essential knowledge is located. They find knowledge that is accurate and appropriate to apply to resolve problems. The next section presents resources provide the starting point for the search for accurate and appropriate information related to safe schools.

Resources for School Leaders, Teachers, Parents, and Community Leaders in Building Safe Schools

The following pages provide an array of resources for the school leader to construct and maintain a safe school. These resources include organizations, Web sites, books, and the identification of centers that make available information, training, or assistance. This list of resources is not inclusive. It serves, however, to facilitate research in discovering existing knowledge that is beneficial to your situation.

Council of Chief State School Officers
1 Massachusetts Avenue, NW/Suite 700
Washington, D.C. 20001-1431
202-408-5505

Council for Basic Education
1319 F Street NW
Washington, D.C. 20004
202-347-4171

National Alliance of Business
1201 New York Ave., NW
Suite 700
Washington, D.C. 20005-3917
202-289-2888

Mexican American Legal
    Defense and Education Fund
634 S. Spring Street
Los Angeles, Calif. 90014
213-629-2512

The National Urban League
500 East 62nd Street
New York, N.Y. 10021-8379
212-310-9000

U.S. Department of Education
400 Maryland Avenue, SW
Washington, D.C. 20202
www.ed.gov

Office of Special Education Programs
www.ed.gov/offices/OSERS/OSEP

Federal Resources for Educational
Excellence (FREE)
www.ed.gov/free

Office of Juvenile Justice and
Delinquency Prevention
www.ncjrs.org/ojjdp

Center for Effective Collaboration
and Practice
www.air-dc.org/cecp/cecp.html

Center for the Study and Prevention
of Violence
http://www.colorado.edu/UCB/
Research/cspv

National School Safety Center
www.nssc1.org

Council of Great City Schools
www.cgcs.org

Institute on Violence and Destructive Behavior
http://interact.uoregon.edu/ivdb/ivdb.html

Centers for Disease Control and Prevention,
Division of Violence Prevention
www.cdc.gov/ncipc/dvp/dvp.htm

National Association of
Secondary School Principals
1904 Association Drive
Reston, Va. 22091
703-860-0220
www.nassp.org

Safe and Drug-Free Schools
Programs Office
www.ed.gov/offices/OESE/SDFS
E-mail: SAFESCHL@ed.gov

Office for Civil Rights
www.ed.gov/offices/OCR

Regional Educational Laboratories
www.nwrel.org/national/index.html

The Justice Information Center
www.ncjrs.org

The Center for Positive Behavior
Intervention and Support
http://stpreos.uoregon.edu/stpweb/pbs/
index.html

Community Anti-Drug Coalitions of
America
901 N. Pitt Street, Suite 300
Alexandria, Va. 22314
703-706-0560

School Mental Health Project/Center
for Mental Health in Schools (UCLA)
http://smhp.psych.ucla.edu

National Education Association
www.nea.org

National Youth Gang Center Behavior
www.iir.com/nygc

Center for Substance Abuse Prevention
(CSAP)
www.samhsa.gov/csap/index.htm

The following on-line federal documents supply relevant research related to effective strategies and tactics in improving school safety. These documents also offer resource information in terms of schools and communities that successfully transformed their schools into safe learning environments.

> *Safe, Drug-Free, and Effective Schools for All Students: What Works*
>   www.air-dc.org/cecp/resources/safe&drug_free/main.htm
> *Early Warning, Timely Response: A Guide to Safe Schools*
>   www.ed.gov/offices/OSERS/OSEP/earlywrn.html
> *Preventing Youth Hate Crime: A Manual for Schools and Communities*
>   www.ed.gov/pubs/HateCrime/start.html
> *Manual to Combat Truancy*
>   www.ed.gov/pubs/Truancy/
> *Creating Safe and Drug-Free Schools: An Action Guide*
>   www.ed.gov.offices/OESE/SDFS/actguid/index.html
> *Recommendations of the Crime, Violence, and Discipline Task Force*,
> NCES 97-581
>   www.ed.gov/NCES

SPECIFIC SAFE SCHOOL STRATEGIES

It is important that the safe school plan meet the needs of the school and its surrounding community. These needs vary greatly from one community to the next, from one school to the next. Over the past two decades, school leaders have seen the development of packaged programs designed to transform their school into a safe school. "Research on the effectiveness of these programs is not plentiful, much of it is technically flawed, and unfortunately, findings are generally inconclusive."[13] The prudent school leader understands that although packaged programs have excellent features, they lack universal application. As part of the school leader's knowledge management process, she recognizes the wisdom in studying these programs to identify aspects applicable to her context.

Reality Therapy (RT)

William Glasser, the developer of reality therapy, believes that responsibility is a fundamental concept to this approach. "Responsibility is the ability to fulfill one's needs, and to do so in a way that does not deprive others of the ability to fulfill their needs."[14] Glasser's program focuses on teachers helping students to understand the consequences of their behavior. The program emphasizes clearly stated and communicated rules, behavior modification contracts, and the involvement of students to discuss the classroom environment.

Reality therapy identifies five basic needs of people: power, love and belonging, freedom, fun/pleasure/enjoyment, and survival. Each person is acting at all times to meet these needs. To meet these needs, reality therapy stresses that people focus on areas they can control, thus empowering the person. The empowered person or student is one who realizes that the only person he can control is himself.[15]

Positive Approach to Discipline (PAD)

Glasser's reality therapy drives the positive approach to discipline. Pat Steffens, an extension family life specialist, asserts:

> A positive approach to discipline helps adults and children work together rather than against each other. It preserves a child's dignity and self-esteem while encouraging cooperative, positive, and loving relationships. Learning to use positive discipline is based upon mutual respect and cooperation, which can have a powerful affect on helping a child develop confidence and a strong self image.[16]

PAD's primary focus is to teach students responsibility. Students learn responsibility through collaboration in developing rules, providing opportunities for success, and using in-school suspension for students who are not able to conform to the process.

Teacher Effectiveness Training (TET)

Teacher effectiveness training provides a process to separate ownership of problems. Teacher ownership of problems as well as student ownership of problems is part of this process. A negotiation and problem-solving process are necessary skills for students to work through problems that often escalate into discipline/behavior issues.

Transactional Analysis (TA)

Transactional analysis is a system of social psychology developed by Eric Berne that examines the relationships within the ego and between individuals.

Transactional analysis studies the interactions of behavior between teachers and students. In order for teachers to be successful in transactional analysis, they need to remain in the Adult ego-state and be able to recognize the ego-state of students around them. Teachers can then recognize the games that students may play in a Child ego-state and teach students to behave in an Adult ego-state.[17]

TA is primarily a counseling tool that assists students in identifying forces influencing their behavior and in making appropriate decisions that results in appropriate behavior change used within the context of the counseling program.

Assertive Discipline

Lee and Marlene Canter developed "Assertive Discipline." The system may be the most widely used discipline program among American schools. It stresses the duty and responsibility of teachers to set accurate and appropriate standards for behavior and stresses holding students accountable for operating within those standards. As such, teachers apply well-defined rules and consequences. As students misbehave, the severity of consequences increases for the student. The Canters believe that an essential element of assertive discipline is positive reinforcement.[18]

Adlerian Psychology

Alfred Adler's work operates on the following principles:

- The person's needs are gestalt-like where the individual's drives, emotions, feelings, and so forth, are all part of the greater organization of the person.
- Each person needs a future orientation to overcome challenges, be competent, be successful, and demonstrate superiority.
- Individuals can determine their unique place and future through generative actions.
- Each person operates in a complex systems web that extends well beyond the family.
- Each person can learn to live in harmony.
- Each person must learn to contribute to society.
- Each person promotes personal and group self-esteem.[19]

These seven principles are inherent in strategies that seek to discover the reasons for a student's inappropriate behavior.

Student Rights

The effective school leader and his team understand student rights. Students have rights defined by the U.S. Supreme Court (see Table 7.4).

APPLICATION OF KNOWLEDGE TO THE SAFE SCHOOL PLAN

The application of knowledge is vital in the development and implementation of a safe school plan. When the school leader frames issues in the context of a window, he can view specific problems in terms of time available for resolution. There is an important distinction between the time required and the time available to resolve problems. The problem may be complex and require substantial time to resolve the problem. Time, however, is a dependent variable. The amount of time available to resolve a problem relates directly to influence and pressures coming from the school community's political context.

Time *available* is a political issue and varies substantially with time *required*. The time required to reduce the number of suspensions may take more than a year as school administrators and faculty work with the community to develop programs to address student needs and increase parent involvement. State requirements related to suspensions may have a different time line. Clearly, classification by the state education department as a problem school because of the high number of suspensions creates political fallout.

For example, Norma Rendone, principal of Salito High School, is under pressure from the state education agency to reduce the number of out-of-school suspensions. Her school surpassed the cutoff level allowed by the state education department. Norma's superintendent told her that continued monitoring by the state department of education was unacceptable. There is a big discrepancy between time required and time available for Norma. She must act within the time available constraints. Likewise, the school leader and his team must act decisively to address the problems based on a time available focus. The school leader and his team operates in the world of political reality and needs to focus on time that is available to resolve an issue that has high public visibility.

Table 7.4 Student Constitutional Rights

Student Right[20]	Explanation
Freedom of association	A student may join any organization he or she chooses in school unless it is illegal or harmful to the public good.
Dress and grooming	Many states now provide legislative power for school districts to mandate uniforms. A good rule of thumb to remember is that students have the right to wear the type of clothes and groom themselves according to individual taste as long as their appearance does not disrupt the educational process, is lewd, obscene, or present a health or safety danger.
Speech and expression	In *Tinker v. Des Moines Independent Community School District*, the Supreme Court gave students protection of the Constitution. As such, students have the right to public expressions, political assertions, and can assert dissatisfaction of the educational system and administrators and/or teachers unless they cause substantial disorder of the educational process.
Suspension	In *Goss v. Lopez*, the Supreme Court held that preceding a suspension school officials must give the student a voiced or written account of the allegations and proof to support the charges leading to suspension. If the student rejects the charges, the student has the right to introduce contrary evidence to the suspending school official. If the student is an ongoing danger, or threat of disruption to the learning process, school officials may immediately remove the student from school and fulfill the legal requirements after the suspension.
Corporal punishment	Twenty-one states ban corporal punishment. In states allowing corporal punishment the physical punishment must be reasonable, necessary, and not excessive.[21] Even in states that permit corporal punishment, local districts have policies that relate directly to its use. The school leader is prudent in following local policies. (My opinion: The use of corporal punishment is a symbol of power, aggression, and violence. It is a poor lesson and one that educators should never use.)
School search	The Fourth Amendment of the Constitution protects students from unreasonable search. Any search must be reasonable. For a search to be reasonable, the school official must have sound grounds given the governing factors, and so forth, that a transgression of school rules or law has occurred. The investigation is appropriate in terms of its scope, intensity, and duration. To warrant a search the school needs to have detected evidence that a rules/law violation was in proceeding: observed evidence of a stolen object; observed evidence of a weapon; observed evidence of drugs, alcohol, or some other prohibited substance; the odor of burning tobacco or cannabis; the student showing influence of alcohol/drugs; the student's confirmation of fault; questionable behavior by the student; implicating testimony submitted by another student or person; the student's fleeing the school.[22]

Table 7.4 Student Constitutional Rights (*Continued*)

Student Right[20]	Explanation
School search *(continued)*	In any event, any search includes witness testimony. The effective school leader uses her intuition to inform her as to whether a search is prudent. Group searches are illegal except in those cases where "the search is 'minimally intrusive' and where the individual's reasonable expectation of privacy is not subject to the discretion of the official in the field."[23] In general, group and strip searches are the cause of needless problems.

Source: This table is adapted from Carolyn Pereira, *Youth and Society Rights and Responsibilities*, 5th ed. (Chicago: Constitutional Rights Foundation, 1994), <http://www.crfc.org/youth.html> (5 April 2000).

There is a difference in time available and time required resolving a wide range of problems. Consider the time needed to resolve the issue of improving the aspiration levels of children from poverty contrasted with preventing guns on campus. Both of these are serious problems. One must be addressed immediately; the other can be addressed over a longer period. The issue of guns on campus is an immediate threat to the safety to every person on campus. That issue must be addressed first. Ranking problems based on the problem's gravity allows the school leader and her team to determine the problem's priority.

Maslow's Hierarchy of Needs

One way to rank problems based on available time is to use Maslow's hierarchy of needs as an applicable standard (see Figure 7.1).[24]

Self-Actualizing

Esteem

Belonging and Love

Safety

Physiological

Figure 7.1   Maslow's Hierarchy of Needs

First Priority: Physiological Needs

Physiological needs refer to food, water, and oxygen. These needs include all that is essential to personal survival. We can interpret physiological needs to refer to an adequate diet that is nutritionally sound, the availability of clean water to drink, and air that is fit to breathe. Physiological needs relate directly to safe school issues. Nutrition experts have long advocated that different types of food affect physical and mental well-being.

At a U.S. Senate hearing in 1977, national experts linked food to the behavior of children. Dr. Bernard Weiss stated:

> Perhaps more pertinent to this committee's mission, food additives now are claimed to contribute to the prevalence of childhood behavioral disorders designated by terms such as hyperactivity, hyperkinesis, and minimal brain dysfunction. Although the diagnostic criteria are amorphous, common elements seem to include elevated aimless activity, difficulty in concentration, clumsiness, and other incipient neurological deficits.[25]

Addressing physiological issues eliminates problems that exist in many contexts. One principal in New England discovered that the heating system had shut down on a Saturday night in January. The temperatures that weekend plummeted to well below zero. On Monday morning, the custodians found that pipes burst throughout the school and that the heating system was no longer functional. It would have been impossible to have school because of the freezing temperatures. The physiological needs of students and teachers would not have been met. No learning would have taken place and much harm would have occurred. It was essential to meet the school community's physiological needs. Applying the window concept to this problem demonstrates the limited available time to address this problem. Cost factors were not an issue as crews worked around the clock to repair the heating system. Physiological issues are important to resolve immediately.

Second Priority: Safety Needs

Safety needs relate to a personal sense of security, stability, or predictability. When the school leader takes care of the safety needs of the school community, she provides a sense of protection and absence of fear, anxiety, or anarchy. She also provides the presence of structure, law, order, and limits. She knows that when people feel safe, they work and relate effectively. When teachers or students feel threatened in classrooms, hallways, stairways, or lavatories, however, their safety needs become a priority. Safety needs are important issues where there is little available time.

The threat to personal safety is at the core of creating a safe school environment. For example, "The Education Department said that in 1996–1997, 6093 students were expelled for bringing a firearm to school—including more than 500 elementary students."[26] In addition, research by the Joyce Foundation reports the disturbing information that 59 percent of students believed that they could "get their hands on a handgun if necessary." Thirty-nine percent of students personally knew someone killed or injured by a firearm, and 22 percent of students believed they would be safer if they carried a handgun if they knew they would be in a fight.[27]

Third Priority: The Need to Belong and to Feel Loved

The third priority is group affiliation needs. The school leader recognizes these needs as reflecting the sense of bonding and belonging. He knows that as important as it is to belong to a group, it is equally important to sense that one is capable of receiving and giving love. Here, the dynamics of the teacher–student relationship make a difference. It is at this level that the school leader and members of his school community commit themselves to each other. It is at this level that the school leader focuses on creating an inclusive school environment. The sense of belongingness emerging from an inclusive school environment leads to solidarity among members. As psychologist and author M. Scott Peck states, "The key to community is the acceptance—in fact, the celebration—of our individual and cultural differences. Such acceptance and celebration—which resolves the problems of pluralism and which can occur only after we learn how to become empty—is also the key to world peace."[28] Creating an inclusive community environment leads to collaborative planning and cooperation in meeting individual and organizational challenges.

Fourth Priority: Esteem Needs

Esteem needs focus on two parallel areas: personal mastery and external recognition. *Personal mastery* refers to one's recognition of personal competence, skills to meet life's challenges, ability to learn new tasks, and the desire to gain further mastery. *External recognition* refers to the respect, affirmation, acknowledgment, and recognition that one gains from others. Personal mastery is reinforced through external recognition. Peter Senge, management expert, states, "People with a high level of personal mastery share several basic characteristics. They have a special sense of purpose that lies behind their visions and goals. They live in a continual learning mode. They are acutely aware of their ignorance, their incompetence, and their growth areas. And they are deeply self-confident."[29] The synergy between personal mastery and external recognition is effective when the recipient of praise recognizes that the praise is well deserved for personal accomplishment.

Fifth Priority: Self-Actualization Needs

Self-actualization is important for all human beings. Maslow states:

> [Self actualization] is an episode, or a spurt in which the powers of the person come together in a particularly efficient and intensely enjoyable way, and in which he is more integrated and less split, more open for experience, more idiosyncratic, more perfectly expressive or spontaneous, or fully functioning, more creative, more humorous, more ego-transcending, more independent of his lower needs, etc. He becomes in these episodes more truly himself, more perfectly actualizing his potentialities, closer to the core of his Being, more fully human.[30]

Becoming self-actualized is a lifetime goal and not necessarily an immediate pursuit. Here the window of available time reaches into the life span of each person within the school community. A healthy school environment nurtures individual pursuit.

Each level of Maslow's hierarchy has a window of available time. The correct application of applying available time is at the heart of competence and the effective implementation of the safe school plan. Competent people and their organizations have an uncanny sense of what to do and when to do it. This contrasts with incompetent people and incompetent organizations that work hard yet remain focused on the wrong issues.

The effective school leader, desiring to focus accurately, reviews issues and problems addressed by the safe school plan. For example, the school leader and her team may identify student attendance, teacher referrals to the office, lack of administrative support, cutting class, number of suspensions, acts of violence, inconsistent communication between teachers and parents, and lack of guidelines as important issues. Applying the window concept to these issues prioritizes the school leader's focus. The window concept identifies where and when to apply long- and short-range projects aligned to the safe school plan. The effective school leader applies short-range strategies to issues such as developing guidelines, eliminating violence, and providing teachers with administrative support (see Table 7.5). A short-range strategy focuses on resolving concrete problems with limited complexity. A long-range strategy resolves global issues with high degrees of complexity such as student attendance, reducing suspensions, and improving communication between teachers and parents. These issues encompass the involvement of multiple groups, community planning, and consensus generation.

The school leader links short-range strategies to long-range strategies. This process is *tagging*. Tagging occurs metaphorically when you imagine shooting an arrow through the right target and seeing the arrow continue to travel straight toward a long-range outcome. The arrow hits a double target. Tagging between short-range actions and long-range strategies allows the school leader to create a situation of strategic coherence.

Table 7.5 Applying the Window Concept to Identified Problems

Issues	Priority	Available Time	Start Time
Poor student attendance	6	One semester	Select planning team within two weeks, give guidelines, set time frame for recommendations.
High teacher referrals of students to the office	5	One marking period	School team will produce a staff development plan and submit it to the faculty for discussion. Meanwhile, faculty will be coached in new guidelines with a focus on identifying staff with skill deficiencies.
Lack of administrative support of teachers	3	One week	Immediately
High number of students cutting classes	4	Three weeks	Immediately
High number of suspensions	8	One year	Based on the approval of strategies by the school board
High number of acts of violence	2	Two weeks	Immediately
Lack of communication between teachers and parents	7	One marking period	Within the first two weeks of school
Lack of discipline guidelines	1	Forty-eight hours	Prior to the start of school

IDENTIFYING APPROPRIATE TARGETS

The effective school leader identifies appropriate targets for short- and long-term safe school strategies. Identifying appropriate targets requires the school leader to take into account the emotional needs of the community. The school leader considers four components:

1. The school leader links safe school initiatives to the improvement of instruction.
2. The school leader links teacher, administrator, parent, and student efforts.
3. The school leader places priority on providing students with immediate feedback regarding performance.
4. The school leader places a priority on communication.

This first component, linking safe school initiatives to the improvement of instruction, is central to the school's primary mission. For instance, instructional time is an essential instructional objective.

As the research literature demonstrates, the degree to which education time is related to student learning depends on the quality of the time. When school schedules maximize the amount of time available for learning; when instructional time is devoted in large part to academic subjects; when classroom time is well managed; and when curriculum and instruction are appropriate and motivating, students can be expected to learn. Under these conditions, increasing time for learning is likely to lead to increased student learning.[31]

One way to increase instructional time is to make sure that students are in class on time. Having students in class for the maximum amount of minutes within the instructional period influences the amount of instructional contact time the teacher has with the students.

Component 2—placing a priority on linking teacher, administrator, parent, and student efforts—is at the heart of establishing a collaborative, school community approach. A North Central Regional Educational Laboratory (NCREL) monograph suggests that collaboration is at the heart of the instructional process. "In collaborative school cultures, the underlying norms, values, beliefs, and assumptions reinforce and support high levels of collegiality, team work, and dialogue about problems of practice."[32] Expanding this notion of collaboration to all aspects of the school culture empowers members of the school community. In this culture, the school leader makes sure the safe school plan is a collaborative effort.

Component 3, placing priority on providing students with immediate feedback regarding performance, is an instructional effort linked to effective coaching. When teachers and administrators give students immediate feedback regarding performance, students have an opportunity to change. This is especially true if teachers and administrators are skilled at breaking dysfunctional patterns and replacing these patterns with constructive patterns.

Component 4, placing priority on communication, eliminates communication gaps. The initiation of effective communication is the responsibility of the school leader and teachers. According to some communication experts, "The beginning of all successful communication is desire — the desire to communicate. This desire cannot be vague and negotiable. It has to be a flint-hard posture of the will, an inner resolution, a firm promise made to ourselves and to others with whom we are trying to relate."[33] Effective communication is the school leader's priority.

There is a difference between short- and long-range goals. Short-range goals provide immediate benefits by building organizational confidence. Long-range goals, while appropriate and essential, act as a compass in guiding the organization toward its vision. Short-range goals, left alone and applied without alignment, act in a sporadic, chaotic fashion. When aligned with long-range goals, short-range goals act as stepping stones. The National Educational Goals Panel identified eight national goal areas:

1. Readiness to learn
2. School completion
3. Student achievement and citizenship
4. Teacher education and professional growth
5. Mathematics and science
6. Adult literacy and lifelong learning
7. Safe and disciplined, alcohol- and drug-free schools
8. Parental participation

These are long-range goals. Each long-range goal identified by the National Educational Goals Panel has a number of short-range goals or indicators. For example, in its first goal, readiness to learn, the panel identified immunizations, preschool participation, and family–child reading and storytelling as part of their overall strategy to achieving their long-range goal.[34] The school leader and her team, when selecting short- and long-range goals, choose goals that benefit the organization.

ACCURATE TARGETING THROUGH EFFECTIVE DECISION MAKING

Effective decision making supports accurate targeting. The school leader and her team will make decisions about programs, people, and policy. Many teams fail because they do not identify the right problem. Even if they identify a problem, they do not consider an array of alternatives as potential solutions to the problem. In effect, a good decision is impossible, if problem identification is inaccurate. If the school leader makes a decision about the wrong problem, then the original problem remains. In many organizations problems recur month after month, year after year, without anyone questioning the decision-making process. There is an underlying assumption in these organizations that crises occur on a repeating basis. One strategy for improving decision making is to apply the medical model of decision making to school decisions.

THE MEDICAL MODEL OF DECISION MAKING

Identifying the right problem is central to accurate decision making. One way to pinpoint the correct problem is to use the model that physicians use to diagnose patients. The same medical technology and theory used by physicians in diagnosing patients can identify problems that affect many schools.

Imagine that a patient walks into the physician's office and tells the physician that she is ill. What is the physician's first response? Does the physician write out a prescription and tell the patient to call back in ten days? No, a physician does something different. Before examining the patient, the physician asks the patient a series of questions. At one level, the physician is analyzing the patient's symptoms. The physician may ask the patient how long she experienced the symptoms. When did she first notice the symptoms? After the physician identifies all symptoms, the physician asks a new series of questions. Simultaneously, the physician is processing the symptoms against the physician's experience and knowledge base. He is automatically rejecting some illnesses and placing others in a set of possibilities. Within the set of potential illnesses, the physician is prioritizing each illness as to its chances of it being the cause of the patient's symptoms. The physician is continually making decisions informed by data. He begins to collect data by examining symptoms, always seeking their potential causes. In effect, the physician is looking for causes.

The greatest source of failure in any decision-making process is the rapid reaction to a problem situation based on the problem's symptoms. The school leader and her team work to become aware of all of the symptoms present in the problem. In a manner similar to that of a physician, they hit the right target by asking the appropriate questions of those experiencing the symptoms. One way the school leader and her team identify causes is to list all symptoms they detect on the left-hand side of a sheet of paper, one after another. Now, the school leader and team identify the causes of each symptom.

Identifying the causes of the symptoms can be soul-searching process. For example, Angie Barreria, principal of Segura High School, had the school team consider the symptoms of high teacher referral of student behavior problems to the office. She asked the team to consider the potential causes of this problem. The team identified several causes: the students' lack of respect, the lack of teacher preparedness within the classroom, teacher inability to manage classroom behavior, student indifference to consequences, and the lack of a systematic process used by teachers to examine these issues. Angie's school team became aware that the primary causes of the problem lie not in the student but in the school professionals. Angie had to use her political skills to assure teachers that the problem was not the teacher but in the lack of training for teachers. Angie's team focused on the problem and not the person. They were able to eliminate the problem.

When the school leader uses the medical model of diagnosing problems, she accurately applies a knowledge base to the symptoms and is likely to focus attention on symptom's cause. Focusing attention to the causes of the symptoms allows the school leader and her team to generate multiple alternatives and select the best possible alternative as the problem solution. This process heightens the chances for a good decision and promotes safe school practices.

SUMMARY

This chapter gives the school leader and her team the knowledge and skills to identify and hit the right target. It frames the identification of the right target within the context of a knowledge base related to safe schools. The school leader identifies strategic targets by understanding the needs of the school community based on Maslow's needs hierarchy. Understanding the needs hierarchy allows the school leader to address important issues as the basis for addressing higher level needs later. Once the school leader determines priorities, she can apply the window concept to each priority, creating a plan of action where she identifies short- and long-range targets. As a result, she optimally utilizes resources. In selecting the right short-range target, the school leader considers the benefits of his actions. The school leader understands that employing this concept generates immediate, positive, school and community feedback. The school leader can apply the medical model as a guide to address safe school issues. Correct use of this model eliminates the repetitive nature of many problems. It frees administrative and teacher time to focus on other, higher-level issues.

Putting It Together: Advancing with Vigilance	✓
Have the members of the school team identified those parts of the knowledge base that are essential to the development of an effective discipline strategy? Do the members of the school team understand timing? Did the school team apply Maslow's needs hierarchy to the school context in determining priorities? Were benefits and impact considered when selecting targets? Did the targets selected for short-range strategies have high benefits? Did the team apply the medical model to the symptoms and causes of the problem? Did the team identify knowledge/abilities and systemic causes? Did the team apply the window concept to identify the time required to solve problems? Did the team communicate its strategies and successes?	

NOTES

1. President William J. Clinton, "Safe, Disciplined and Drug-Free Schools," *Call to Action for American Education in the 21st Century* (1997), <http://www.ed.gov/updates/PresEDPlan/part7.html> (5 April 2000).

2. *Early Warning, Timely Response: A Guide to Safe Schools*, referenced ed., Center for Effective Collaboration and Practice (1999), <http://www.air-dc.org/cecp/guide/annotated.htm> (5 April 2000).

3. "Toward a Caring School Culture," *Addressing Barriers to Learning* 3, no. 2 (Spring 1998), School Mental Health Project, UCLA <http://smhp.psych.ucla.edu/lesson32.htm> (5 April 2000).

4. "Curriculum Content for Enhancing Social and Emotional Functioning," *Addressing Barriers to Learning* 2, no. 2 (Spring 1997), School Mental Health Project, UCLA, <http://smhp.psych.ucla.edu/lesson22.htm> (5 April 2000).

5. Emanuel Hurwitz, "Critical Issue: Developing and Maintaining Safe Schools," North Central Regional Educational Laboratory (1996), <http://www.ncrel.org/sdrs/areas/issues/envrnmnt/drugfree/sa200.htm> (5 April 2000).

6. "What Parents Can Do," *Annual Report on School Safety* (October 1998), <http://www.ed.gov/pubs/AnnSchoolRept98/parent.html> (5 April 2000).

7. Family/School Partnerships, "Developing Family/School Partnerships: Guidelines for Schools and School Districts," the National Coalition for Parent Involvement in Education, <http://www.ncpie.org/ncpieguidelines.html> (28 June 2000).

8. Kathleen Cotton, "Schoolwide and Classroom Discipline," *School Improvement Research Series (SIRS), Close-Up #9* (December 1990), Northwest Regional Educational Laboratory <http://www.nwrel.org/scpd/sirs/5/cu9/html> (3 March 1999).

9. R. Stephens, "National Trends in School Violence: Statistics and Prevention Strategies," in *School Violence Intervention: A Practical Handbook*, ed. Arnold P. Goldstein and Jane C. Conoley (New York: Guilford, 1997), 72–90.

10. Stephens, "National Trends in School Violence," 72–90.

11. Kai Larsen, Claire McInerney, Corinne Nyquist, Aldo Santos, and Donna Silsbee, *Learning Organizations* (1996) <http://home.nycap.rr.com/klarsen/learnorg/> (5 April 2000).

12. Karl M. Wiig, *Knowledge Management: The Central Management Focus for Intelligent-Acting Organizations* (Chicago: Applied Symboliz, 1994).

13. Cotton, *School Improvement Research Series*.

14. William Glasser, *Reality Therapy: A New Approach to Psychiatry* (New York: Harper & Row, 1975), 15.

15. "Reality Therapy and Choice Theory," *Rogha*, <http://www.angelfire.com/ab/brightminds/tReality.html> (5 April 2000).

16. Pat Steffens, "Positive Approach to Discipline," *Neb Guide* no. G93-1190-A (November 1995), <http://www.ianr.unl.edu/pubs/family/g1190.htm> (5 April 2000).

17. Gene Van Tassel, "Classroom Management," Brains.org Research Applications, <http://www.brains.org/classroom_management.htm> (5 April 2000).

18. Lee Canter, "Assertive Discipline and the Search for the Perfect Classroom," *Young Children* 43 (1988): 2.

19. Heinz L. Ansbacher, "Summary of Alfred Adler's Individual Psychology," *North American Society of Adlerian Psychology* <http://www.alfredadler.org/ip.htm> (5 April 2000).

20. These examples relate to students' rights. They are not inclusive of all students' rights. The explanation endeavors to be accurate, but is not a legal recommendation. The reader should ask advice from his school attorney before acting.

21. American Civil Liberties Union, "Is My Teacher Allowed to Hit Me?" ACLU Department of Public Education, <http://www.aclu.org/students/slfair.html> (5 April 2000).

22. National Association of Attorneys General School Search Checklists (1999), <http://www.keepschoolssafe.org/check.htm> (23 April 1999).

23. Ann Majestic, Jonathon Blumberg, Ruth Dowling, and Tharrington Smith, "Legal and Policy Issues in Curbing Violence in Schools," *Legal Guidelines for Curbing School Violence* (1995), <http://www.keepschoolssafe.org/leg.htm> (5 April 2000).

24. Abraham Maslow, *Toward a Psychology of Being,* 2nd ed. (New York: Van Nostrand, 1968).

25. Statement of Dr. Bernard Weiss, professor of radiation biology and biophysics, Environmental Health Sciences Center, University of Rochester School of Medicine and Dentistry, Rochester, N.Y., at the hearing before the Select Committee on Nutrition and Human Needs of the United States Senate. Ninety-Fifth Congress, First Session, 22 June 1977 (Washington, D.C.: U.S. Government Printing Office).

26. Gordon Witkin, Mike Tharp, Joannie Schrof, Thomas Toch, and Christy Scattarella, "Again," *U.S. News* (1998), <http://www.usnews.com/usnews/issue/980601/1shoo.htm> (5 April 2000).

27. The Joyce Foundation, *LH Research,* National School Safety Center, Westlake, Village, Calif. <http://www.nssc1.org> (10 April 2000).

28. M. Scott Peck, *The Different Drum: Community and Peace Making* (New York: Touchstone, 1987), 161.

29. Peter Senge, *The Fifth Discipline: The Art and Practice of the Learning Organization* (New York: Doubleday, 1990), 142.

30. Maslow, *Toward a Psychology of Being,* 97–98.

31. Julie Aronson, Joy Zimmerman, and Lisa Carlos, "Improving Student Achievement by Extending School: Is It Just a Matter of Time?" PACE Medial Education Writers Seminar (1998), <http://www.wested.org/wested/papers/timeandlearning/4_implicationsPV.html> (6 April 2000).

32. Kent Peterson and Richard Brietzke, "Building Collaborative Cultures: Seeking Ways to Reshape Urban Schools," North Central Regional Educational Laboratory—Urban Monograph Series (1994), <http://www.crel.org/sdrs/areas/issues/educatrs/leadrshp/le0pet.htm> (10 April 2000).

33. John Powell and Loretta Brady, *Will the Real Me Please Stand Up? 25 Guidelines for Good Communication* (Allen, TX: Tabor, 1985), 18.

34. National Educational Goals Panel, "National Educational Goals: Building a Nation of Learners," (1993), <http://www.negp.gov/issues/publication/coalitiondocs/473.html> (10 April 2000).

CHAPTER EIGHT

Reducing the Risk

Principals, teachers, parents, and members of the community feel bewildered by reports of violent behavior in schools. Community members, suffering from unexpected acts of violence, seek to understand why the violence happened. Little by little, they piece together a complex puzzle that points to the motivation behind the acts of violence. In most cases, there is a growing realization that they could have prevented the violence by reducing the risk. This chapter is about reducing the risk of potential violence by creating a process that identifies and integrates at-risk students into the school community. The school leader's task is to identify at-risk students and implement strategies that integrate these students into the school community.

In this chapter, you will:

- apply several strategies to identify at-risk students;
- understand the implications of isolation, powerlessness, and meaninglessness in the at-risk student's life;
- learn how to interrupt reinforcing feedback that accelerates the at-risk student's sense of isolation, powerlessness, and meaninglessness;
- learn how to promote reinforcing feedback that accelerates intellectual, physical, and emotional health among all students, particularly among at-risk students;
- understand the complex nature of systems affecting the life of the at-risk student; and
- understand how to gain parent cooperation in reducing the level of alienation in their at-risk child.

Prevention of violent acts is an essential component to any safe school strategy. Educators recognize the importance of prevention and implement intervention strategies as early as preschool and elementary years with children who are at risk for failing, developing behavioral problems, and dropping out of school. The Pennsylvania School Study Council's report, "Beyond Zero Tolerance: Alternative Strategies to Suspension and Expulsion," asserts, "The first steps in prevention involve developing a caring relationship between educator and child, teaching children to deal with difficult issues that may be beyond their control, encouraging all students to participate in school activities, and establishing high expectations for all students."[1]

Yet, even with the focus on prevention, violence happens. Are we powerless to prevent violence, or have we failed to identify the right paradigm to address this issue? We are not powerless. Any sense of powerlessness that we feel regarding the prevention of school violence has its cause in our failure to reframe the issue and consider alternative paradigms. One way of regaining a sense of powerfulness is to change the language that we use to define issues. Peter Senge, author of the *Fifth Discipline,* tells us that language is perception. The words we use create mental images regarding a person, situation, or context. If we change the words, we change the image.[2]

LABELING

As educators, we know that labels have both beneficial and deleterious effects. Words that describe a student as gifted and promising create an image in that student's mind that he or she has special talent. Words that describe a student as at-risk, a troublemaker, or a gangster create an image in that student's mind that he or she is antisocial. Henry Levin, director of the Center for Educational Research at Stanford University, states:

> Research tells us that at birth these children have the same need for love and affection, the same developing curiosity, the same physiological requirements and so on as children who are not in at-risk situations. How should we think of them? We had best think of them as children like all children. They have the needs of children, and that's where we have to begin.[3]

One of the first steps in reclaiming power and in reducing the impact of at-risk students is to stop labeling the students we consider at risk.

Labels are part of our language and help us to classify and sort objects so that we make sense out of our world. It is important to give a piece of furniture a label as a chair and another piece of furniture the label of lamp. It helps us to communicate to each other about particular pieces of furniture. In general, we understand what a person is talking about when they use the word *chair* or the word *lamp*. Applying the same constructs to human beings creates problems. Labels get in the way of understanding human beings. We know from our national history that the use of labels fostered feelings of racial superiority. We know that was wrong. We also know that labeling is not always accurate. Some teachers, for example, labeled Edison and Einstein, both geniuses, as stupid.

Labeling is imprecise because language is imprecise. It is imprecise because we also attach emotions or feelings to the word or label. Thus, a four-letter word such as *fire* may mean warmth, cooking, something spiritual, or a traumatic event. The meaning and emotion we attach to a word has its basis in our experience. Since we have different experiences, our perception of language is different.

When the school leader understands her reliance on labels, she becomes aware of the communication problems caused by labeling. The school leader can determine her reliance on labels by answering the following questions.

- Do I use labels to identify students?
- Do I use labels to identify teachers?
- Do I use labels to identify subgroups of students?
- Do I use labels to identify the quality of the student?
- Do I use labels when dealing with parents?
- Do I use labels when referring to the community?
- Do I use labels when referring to the school board?
- Do I use labels when referring to the school administration?

Exploring these questions with the school team helps to raise awareness of the extent that school community members use labels to communicate. For example, what labels do teachers and school leaders use when talking about parents? Do teachers and school leaders refer to parents as single parents, working parents, pushy parents, or achievement-oriented parents? What meaning do we give to each of these classifications? Making the distinction between the use of essential labels and nonessential labels is an important first step in working with students labeled at risk.

Essential labels are necessary for organizational and communication purposes. It is important to consider the consequences of the application of any label. What does the label *gifted and talented* mean? Does it mean that the students selected for a gifted and talented program are academically and intellectually gifted and talented? Does it mean that students not in gifted and talented programs lack academic and intellectual talent? What message does this label send to students, teachers, and parents? How does this message affect the motivation of students or the expectations of teachers and parents?

Students often use labels to separate themselves. Teachers and school leaders hear students refer to each other as nerds, jocks, geeks, or druggies. When students choose to belong to one of these groups, they accept the values and labels associated with them. On the one hand, students enter into a small group and benefit from the acceptance the small group offers. On the other hand, if the small group places a priority on antisocial values, isolates itself from the mainstream, and sees itself as repressed, its members are at risk as well as others working in the same environment. The danger for school leaders is the association of the at-risk potential with antisocial, abnormally rebellious groups.

School leaders unwittingly collaborate with these groups when they use labels and identify members as different from mainstream students. This exacerbates the group's sense of uniqueness, provides group members with recognized status, and reinforces the group's values in the minds of group members as well as faculty and students not belonging to the group.

The irony with labeling is that in the application of labels, the school leader and teacher focus attention on the students with the label. Since we can only focus on a single object at any given moment, we fail to observe mainstream students who display at-risk symptoms. In essence, given the conditions prevalent in contemporary society in terms of social pressures, changing mores, and continued questioning of traditional values, it is important to see all students as being at risk. The studious honor student is as likely to lose control as is a student identified as having a behavior disorder. *All* students are potentially at risk.

When school leaders and teachers operate from the premise that all students are at risk, they can devise strategies to reduce the risk among all students. A beginning step is to become aware of how faculty, school leaders, staff, and students exacerbate existing problems. For example, a teenager, sexually abused as a child, may react defiantly toward a teacher who has the same gender as the abuser. The teacher has no knowledge of the teenager's sexual abuse history. The teenager, who represses the sexual abuse, is not conscious of its occurrence. The teacher, unclear about the teenager's history, refers the student to the office. The student's rage toward authority escalates. The principal suspends the student. The principal's action removes the symptoms, but the cause still exists. Each student carries a history. This hidden history is a primary source of human motivation.

Students also contribute to the growth of an at-risk environment. Students often engage in practices of isolating peers who appear different by bullying, isolating, and tormenting tactics. This behavior sets the stage for the receiver of the abusive behavior to respond through flight, dropping out of school, truancy, or fight in the form of covert or overt reprisals. When school leaders and teachers ignore these practices, a social group system develops among students. Overlooking student-generated caste systems sanctions the values espoused by the ruling social groups. School leaders and teachers become coconspirators with students in ruling social groups.

Two strategies can help reduce the risk for violence and create a safe school environment: (1) developing a sense of community and (2) diagnosing at-risk symptoms present in students and immediately treating those symptoms. Many schools opt for increased vigilance strategies. They hire security to patrol the hallways, require uniforms, implement zero-tolerance policies, and use immediate referrals to alternative school settings for specific behaviors. These and similar strategies are effective in eliminating the symptoms associated with unsafe school environments. They do not treat the cause of the symptoms. Simultaneously building a sense of community and treating at-risk symptoms is an effective answer to many of the causes of school violence.

BUILDING A SENSE OF COMMUNITY

Three essential questions must be answered in building a sense of community:

1. How do we define community?
2. How do we build a sense of community?
3. How do we maintain a sense of community over time?

Understanding community and its context is at the core of building a safe school. The leader's responsibility is to create a sense of inclusion among school members and to reduce the impact of the variables that contributes to generating at-risk characteristics. Parker Palmer, an authority on community building, suggests four primary characteristics of community:[4]

- Occupying a common space
- Sharing common resources
- Enjoying common opportunities
- Learning to live together

The first aspect is that members of the school community, although representing a panoply of backgrounds, occupy common space. Students may be affluent or poor, with traditional or nontraditional backgrounds, or members of a majority or minority culture. Students may have parents who care for them or parents who abuse them. Some students have lofty goals, while others drift without clear direction or purpose. Teachers and school leaders need to reflect in order to identify the disparity found among students. In the end, regardless of background, students—whether in the classroom, hallways, cafeteria, or athletic fields—share the same space.

The second aspect reflects that those who occupy a common space also share the resources available in that space. The resources are as varied as classroom space, library resources, lunchroom space, locker space, recreational space, lavatory space, paper, books, supplies, and bus seats. This brief listing scratches the surface of the resources shared by members of the school community. The willingness of the members of the community to share resources and to apply the resources to the best interests of each member is an important part of developing a healthy sense of community.

The third aspect of community, enjoying common opportunities, expands the notion of sharing. Emerging out of any organization are opportunities that fulfill the human spirit by allowing the member to use his or her potential to its fullest capacity. When each member of the school community understands that the organization wants the member to succeed, the member moves into an optimistic, hope-filled environment. Many school leaders, teachers, and students have the experience of being in a school environment where only a select few have opportunities. A healthy community discovers that there are sufficient opportunities for each member.

Learning to live together is the fourth characteristic of community; it is the glue of community. Learning to live together means that members allow for individual differences, discover ways to work through disagreements, establish common rules, and recognize the inherent gift that each member brings to the community. Learning to live together has its foundation in the ability of community members to build and sustain meaningful relationships with each other. It is through these meaningful relationships that members generate creative ideas, turn the ideas into substantive plans, have the capacity to implement the plans, and sustain the plans.

Schools that create an inclusive sense of community generate an environment that retards the growth of at-risk behaviors. The practices in the previous chapters, when followed, build an inclusive community. More important, rather than a set of prescribed ideas and actions, an inclusive community derives its strength from the belief system and underlying philosophy of school leaders and teachers.

Community building is carefully planned, well constructed, and integrated into every action. Community is either present in a school or absent. When it is absent, multiple small communities grow to fill the void left by the absence of the larger community. Many of these small communities have constructive elements, but others operate with a destructive philosophy. Sometimes this destructive philosophy turns inward, and we read about student suicides, drug abuse, and other similar self-hatred events. At other times, this destructive philosophy turns itself outward with attacks against unsuspecting members of the school community. This occurred at Columbine High School, site of the mass killings in 1999, in Littleton, Colorado. *Time* magazine reported the existence of one of these small communities that turned violent:

> In an odd way, I think much can be explained by the trench coats, not because they are long and black and what the kids call Gothic, but because they look alike; they conceal differences. People who are attracted to clans and cults seek to lose their individuality and discover power and pride in a group. As individuals, the killers, Eric Harris and Dylan Klebold, were vulnerable, taunted by the other tribes in school—the cliques, the athletes—as geeks and nerds. "He just put a gun to my head," a girl reported. "And he started laughing and saying it was all because people were mean to him last year."[5]

CREATING A SPIRIT OF COMMUNITY

A spirit of community arises out of the school's membership. School leaders create a spirit of community when they implement the following four actions:

1. Act with integrity.
2. Move toward dialogue.

3. Bring everyone into the discussion.
4. Respect each person's values and viewpoint.

Acting with Integrity

Integrity indicates a sense of wholeness. This sense of wholeness links a person's intentions with his actions. In effect, the person's actions portray his beliefs and values. This is true of individuals and organizations. To the extent that we act with integrity, others can trust us. When the school leader's values and beliefs express the values and beliefs of the members of the school community, and each action is consistent with those beliefs, then environmental trust develops. Out of environmental trust comes a belief that each person in the organization has value, that each person's views deserve respect, and that each person is important and indispensable to the organization.

Moving toward Dialogue

Physicist David Bohm makes a distinction between discussion and dialogue. He states that the root for *discussion* and *percussion* are the same. The purpose of a discussion is to impose ideas, concepts, and beliefs on others. Discussion is a competitive activity. Conversely, dialogue, rather than a competitive activity, is a cooperative activity in which both parties seek understanding and reconciliation to a common viewpoint. Dialogue leads to the discovery of common ground.[6]

The effective school leader makes dialogue a priority. Dialogue occurs in the principal's office, classroom, teacher lounge, and student cafeteria when people commit themselves to listening non-judgmentally, seeking to understand, and asking questions to deepen understanding. In many ways, entering into dialogue leads a person to question existing outdated views. The best way to create a dialogue-driven environment is to gain commitment from school leaders, faculty, and students to acquiring dialoguing skills.

Bringing Everyone into the Discussion

A spirit of community is inclusive. In inclusive school communities, the organization encourages community, member participation, and a sense of invitation. Participation is an integral part of inclusion because it brings all members of the organization to the table. There is no exclusion in a community-driven organization. Full participation and inclusion often result in chaos. It is out of chaos, however, that the bonds of community strengthen and the organization thrives.

Many organizations make the mistake of avoiding the chaos associated with real community. These organizations deny the existence of hidden issues out of the mistaken notion that tranquility results in community. Denial of real issues actually leads to friction and results in disunion and the development of exclusionary practices.

Respecting Each Person's Values and Viewpoint

Genuine community has its foundation in the respect that members have for each other and each other's viewpoint. M. Scott Peck states, "In genuine community there are no sides. The members have learned how to give up cliques and factions. They have learned how to listen to each other and how not to reject each other."[7] Members gain respect by listening nonjudgmentally. They realize that each person owns a piece of the truth and not the whole truth, and it is through combining the pieces of truth that a clearer picture of reality develops. School leaders who encourage and facilitate this behavior build a sense of community that fosters an environment where at-risk behavior is kept at a minimum. In this environment, students normally associated with at-risk behavior shed their need to form separate groups, their cliques become merged with other groups, and all work toward creating a safe school environment.

A sense of community requires leadership, commitment, and persistence to overcome past hurts and inertia. As a result, community building is a time- and energy-consuming process. As this process develops momentum, the school leader and faculty can identify and work with students who feel excluded from the existing school environment.

IDENTIFYING STUDENTS PREDISPOSED TO BE AT RISK

How do we identify students who have a predisposition to be at risk without labeling them as such? Roger Fisher and William Ury of the Harvard Negotiating team suggest an answer:[8] separate the student from the problem. When we do so, we can be hard on the problem and soft on the student. This approach means that the student is not the problem. The student's environment, background, patterns of thinking and behaving become the problem. Thus, the behavior, environment, history, or emotional condition causes the at-risk conditions rather than the student. This distinction makes a big difference. We now identify conditions. Rather than fixing students, we eliminate conditions that are the cause of violent, risk-prone behavior.

IDENTIFYING AT-RISK CAUSES

Identifying the at-risk behaviors, environment, history, emotional, or biological conditions is a complex task since people respond differently to similar stimuli. For example, one student from a low socioeconomic background becomes overwhelmed with the poverty and other conditions associated with his neighborhood. He drops out of school and joins a gang. This student eventually becomes involved in criminal activity. Before long, he is caught, tried, and convicted. Another student, from the same neighborhood with a similar poverty level, becomes motivated to get an education and move his family out of poverty. He graduates, goes to college, and becomes a doctor. Two students with similar stimuli respond differently. The student's response to the stimuli causes the at-risk behavior.

Students respond to stimuli based on response patterns that they acquired from experience and socialization from parents and culture. Students learn these response patterns by modeling behavior they observe in their homes, social groups, or other people who are influential in their lives. These response patterns become structured ways of acting. Over time, as the student practices these structured patterns, the patterns become engrained and the student's response becomes automatic. The student, when presented with the appropriate stimuli, will act in a predictable manner. For example, one student, when criticized, becomes angry and attacks the person making the criticism. Another student, when criticized, becomes depressed and withdraws with a damaged ego. A third student, when criticized, becomes motivated and seeks to use the criticism to improve performance. Each student responds predictably. Each student is unaware of her motivation and the reasons for the response. In this case, only the third student is not at risk. The first student is at risk to respond violently toward the person making the criticism. The second student is at risk to respond violently toward herself. Understanding the student's motivation is important to school leaders and teachers. Once school leaders and teachers understand the student's motivation, they can help to increase the student's awareness of her response patterns. This task begins with an understanding of basic personality types.

BASIC PERSONALITY TYPES

According to the famed psychologist Karin Horney, there are three basic personality types: movement toward people, movement against people, and movement away from people.[9] Although everyone has aspects of each of the three personality types, one type dominates our behavior. Each personality type describes our basic motivations; it explains why we do what we do.

In many ways, our personality is the internal compass that we use to guide us through life. When our compass is working well, we live normal lives, we deal effectively with problems, and we meet with success. When our compass is not working well, we create problems, make poor decisions, and constantly confront failure. Each personality has the capacity to act as an effective compass or to act as a defective compass. At-risk behavior arises from those with defective compasses.

Understanding basic personality types provides school leaders and teachers with the power to help students refocus their reference points. Each personality type has its positive, empowering, constructive side. Likewise, each personality type has its negative, disempowering, destructive side. Each school leader, teacher, student, or parent allows one side of her personality to dominate and direct her future. The personality types as described here focus on students and the at-risk potential that exists when they frame their views of the world from the negative, disempowering, and destructive side of their personalities.

Type 1: Movement toward Others

This student is the follower, constantly looking for affiliation with external groups. He needs acceptance. If acceptance does not come from mainstream groups, the student seeks acceptance from groups outside the mainstream. The student anchors behavior to norms established by the group with whom he seeks affiliation. A type 1 student who associates with students who have a drug dependency will likely develop a drug dependency even when confronted with the detrimental effects of drugs. The type 1 student's need for affiliation far outweighs the student's concern for his body. His basic requirement of having to be needed is unmet in the traditional school environment and the student's home. Unwittingly, the student finds this need met by a group whose norms encourage at-risk behavior.

Behavior traits associated with the type 1 student with potential for affiliation with at-risk groups include these:

- Nonassertive for own needs
- Seeks affiliation with a powerful leader
- Needs to be affiliated with some kind of social group
- Has a tendency toward low self-esteem
- Does not recognize own capabilities
- Has a limited ability to refuse requests
- Is fearful of being disliked

Type 2: Movement against Others

This student is aggressive. The student's aggression manifests itself in bullying other students and directing physical and emotional abuse toward peers, teachers, and others in authority. If provoked, he will move toward physical attacks. This student, like his counterpart who moves toward people for affiliation, needs to be with people. This student, however, unlike his counterpart, seeks followers. He is not a follower. If he is not the leader, he will challenge the person in the leadership position. It does not matter if it is a gang, football team, or classroom; he will seek to dominate. In his desire to dominate, he will continually probe those in authority for signs of weakness. If the person in authority does not stand up to this student, the student loses respect for the person. When publicly confronted, the student, fearing the opinion of his peers, must challenge and respond with escalating aggression. This behavior occurs in classrooms where this type of student, when confronted by the teacher, becomes increasingly violent, putting the teacher and other students at risk. These students frequently come from physically abusive homes. In these environments, they learned that power rules and those with power protect themselves from being hurt or humiliated.

Behavior traits associated with type 2 students with potential for affiliation with at-risk groups are as follows:

- Needs to be the center of attention
- Is likely to explode violently

- Carries large amounts of suppressed and repressed anger
- Projects anger and insecurity onto others, especially authority figures
- Uses other people to achieve personal ends
- Enjoys risky behavior
- Needs to challenge authority and will find excuses to challenge authority

Type 3: Movement Away from Others

This student is the loner. She has few friends. She does not trust other people and seldom shares her story with others. Her stance as a loner projects the appearance of an introvert. She will sit in the back of the classroom, not engage in class discussion unless directed by the teacher, and, because of a perceived aloofness, is often the butt of verbal teasing and tormenting by peers. This student's behavior often creates a cycle that reinforces the needs to move away from others and to seek safety in an inner world. This inner world frequently involves into a fantasy world where the student seeks escape. The student fantasizes resolving problems, achieving goals, and moving to exotic places where she will not have to deal with the mundane issues that infect her life. The more she moves into this fantasy world, the more she moves away from those in her immediate environment. When she interacts with her environment, she realizes how poorly this real environment compares to her fantasy world. She tries to maintain her isolation by balancing a passive-aggressive response to her environment. Her primary response is to be passive. She wants to operate on a live-and-let-live premise. When others continue to intrude, she, unexpectedly, becomes aggressive. Her aggressive response is frequently disproportional to the stimulus. Other students, teachers, parents, and school leaders are not ready for the attack. Literally, the stimulus is the straw that broke the camel's back. This aggressive response is as likely to be turned on her as it is to be turned on to others. As a result, this type of student, more than the other two types, is likely to commit suicide. The tragedy is that the student's cries for help fall unheard since her introverted behavior rejects attention.

Behavior traits associated with type 3 students with potential for affiliation with at-risk groups are these:

- Seeks continuous privacy
- Broods over the lack of fulfillment received in the current environment
- Creates a fantasy world
- Seldom seeks help or offers to help

- Operates from a passive-aggressive stance
- Lives in a fantasy world that encourages peer rejection
- Creates elaborate fantasy plots to get even with others

WHAT CAN SCHOOL LEADERS DO?

Proactive preparation is essential for the school leaders to create a safe school. Proactive preparation means that the school leader works to make sure teachers understand the traits associated with a student's propensity to associate with at-risk behavior or become immersed in an at-risk environment. Proactive preparation begins with awareness of the current reality. Speaking about the importance of awareness of current reality as an essential component of personal mastery, Senge states, "They see current reality as an ally, not an enemy. They are deeply inquisitive, committed to continually seeing reality more and more accurately."[10]

Awareness after the fact is too late to alter the behavior. The earlier the effective school leader becomes aware of what is happening, the quicker he responds and prevents the potential escalation of events to an at-risk situation. Awareness on the part of the school leader creates a sense of urgency. Urgency to action indicates the window within which it is important to take preventive action. Each level of awareness links itself to a level of urgency. The level of urgency determines the type and intensity of response. Table 8.1 provides levels of awareness and their corresponding urgency.

Awareness is difficult in situations that rapidly change. School leaders and teachers need to reflect continually on current reality. As they consider student behavior and the school's context, they need to remember that actions speak louder than words. Each student expresses his actions to align with his personality. School leaders need to guard against only recognizing loud and attention grabbing actions. They also need to be aware of silent, seemingly unexpressed actions. They need to respond to any action or activity before it leads to disastrous consequences. School leaders gain awareness by asking important questions such as these:

- Are any of my students acting different than they have in the past?
- Is any student exhibiting behavior associated with potential at-risk situations or at-risk activities?

- Am I aware of the varieties of behavior of each of my students?
- Are there any students that I am ignoring?
- Are there silent calls for help that I missed?

We compare the vigilant awareness needed by school leaders and teachers to that of the air controller. The air controller constantly monitors her radar screen, guiding aircraft toward their destination. She places each plane in context with her assigned environment. She leaves nothing to chance: she knows she has the safety of thousands of human beings in her hands. The vigilant school leader and teacher respond the same way to their environment.

Table 8.1 Levels and Urgency of Student Behavior

Level	Urgency
Level 1: Awareness of level 1 behavior indicates the student does not display traits that may harm self or others. The student's behavior indicates dependency, excessive aggression, or withdrawal.	When school leaders or teachers recognize level 1 behavior, an intervention team meets to identify strategies to prevent the student moving into higher urgency levels. Teachers and school leaders monitor the situation. The basic intervention is to restructure the student's environment to break emerging behavior patterns.
Level 2: Awareness of level 2 behavior indicates a growing concern related to the student's behavior. The student's actions, although not yet serious, raise concern because of their consistency.	Level 2 behavior requires an urgent response. The student's environment and his awareness of his behavior are crucial to modifications. The response team involves the student, parents, and teachers to identify creative coping strategies.
Level 3: Awareness of level 3 behavior should cause an alarm to go off for school leaders. The student is at a point where she is a potential danger to herself or others. The student makes actual or implied threats of violence directed toward self or others. The student may also threaten some type of behavior such as running away. The silent cry of an implied threat in an English assignment is as critical as the overt threat made toward another person.	Level 3 behavior demands an immediate reaction. The student may need to be restrained and removed to alternative setting or placed in an environment where mental health professionals work with the student and family to resolve the issues provoking the behavior. School leaders and teachers do not have the skills to help students expressing level three behavior. School leaders, recognizing their limitations, seek immediate intervention assistance.

SCHOOL LEADER RESOURCES

School leaders and teachers are instructional leaders. Training to be an instructional leader taught the school leader and the teacher to understand curriculum, teaching, and creating an environment that motivates students to learn. The changing context in contemporary society requires the school leader and teacher to move beyond traditional boundaries of instructional leadership toward a greater understanding of human behavior. Rather than see these two fields as separate entities, it is better to frame them as converging, dynamic fields that influence each other. This section presents a series of resources designed to expand reference points. These resources are not all-inclusive but simply are meant to stimulate further research and inquiry into human behavior.

School leaders, teachers, and parents need to incorporate both left- and right-brain awareness if they are to act as a resource to their children. Brain research tells us that the left hemisphere of our brain is the place of logic, reasoning, and rational thinking. The right hemisphere of our brain is the place of intuition, creativity, and integration of multiple perspectives. We can use this information to prevent children from moving deeper into an at-risk environment. Our logical, reasoning side allows us to be creating environments that require personal discipline. They are environments, formed by understanding and compassion, where students learn personal boundaries and how to interact with other members of society. Our intuitive side tells us when it is not working. It tells us that something is wrong, even when our logical side is not aware that the logical process is falling apart. In this context, the American Academy of Child and Adolescent Psychiatry provides us with a set of indicators, when evident in children, that require an adult response:[11]

Younger Children

- A significant drop in school performance
- Low grades in school, even when the child appears to be trying hard
- Excessive anxiety showing itself in refusal to go to school, go to bed, or participate in activities normal for the child's age
- Prolonged and frequent temper tantrums
- Growing aggressiveness toward others and authority figures
- Hyperactivity: fidgeting and constant movement that appears excessive for age and context

Preadolescents and adolescents

- A significant drop in school performance
- Signs of substance abuse: alcohol or drug use
- Growing inability to cope with small problems and daily activities
- Observable changes in sleeping and/or eating habits
- Growing complaints of physical problems
- Excessive aggressive behavior, especially toward authority and others
- Excessive passive behavior (e.g., running away from facing problems)
- Observed periods of depression or negative moods and attitude
- Preoccupation with death or obsession with cult-related activities

It is the adult's awareness of these behaviors in the student that is important. When the adult is aware of the behavior, the adult is in a position to respond accurately and appropriately. An accurate response requires the recognitions of the problem (the symptoms), the collection of additional data (search for the cause of the symptoms), and an evaluation of the data (seeking the source of the cause of the problem). If school leaders, teachers, and parents respond solely to the symptoms, then they run the risk of the child pretending the problem is resolved. When the child changes context, the problem emerges again. This type of response is common because it brings immediate results; however, the results seldom produce a long lasting effect.

RISK ASSESSMENT

Risk assessment is frequently associated with actuary tables, NASA sending a space shuttle into orbit, or reference to environmental hazards, but it is also important for school leaders. Risk assessment can significantly reduce the level of risk to students, teachers, and school leaders. Conducting a risk assessment creates an awareness of existing conditions that contribute to an unsafe environment. In essence, a risk assessment defines the prospect of undesirable affects when in a specific environment.[12] We express the level of risk as a fraction ranging from 0 to 1.0. When the risk is 1.0, there is complete assurance that the event associated with the risk will occur.

The following example shows the usefulness of the risk assessment: A student who verbally abuses a teacher each time the teacher publicly criticizes her has a risk of 1.0 when the teacher publicly criticizes the student. If the same student verbally abused only female teachers and we know that the student has only male teachers, the risk is much lower, perhaps as low as 0.2.

Using the notion of risk assessment allows us to reduce the risk of self or projected forms of violent or abusive behavior. Effective use of risk assessment has four central components. First, the school administration identifies threshold standards for behavior. Second, the members of the school community develop an awareness of a person nearing threshold behavior. Third, the school leader and her team maintain an ongoing assessment and monitoring of potential risk behavior. Finally, an understanding of the synergistic effect of divergent forces can move a student or other member of the school community from low risk to high risk, creating a volatile situation.

IDENTIFYING THRESHOLD STANDARDS FOR BEHAVIOR

Different in each school community, *threshold standards of behavior* represent the degree to which the school community chooses to tolerate specific behaviors. For example, a teacher pays little attention to a student who does not cause any disturbance but contributes little to the class. The threshold on this behavior becomes operable only when the teacher recognizes that the student is in attendance but not participating in class. In another classroom, the teacher has a high expectation that all students will participate in the class. This teacher's threshold is significantly lower than that of her colleagues. When the student withdraws, the teacher reacts and draws the student back into the flow of classroom activity.

Threshold standards operate in every school and organization. Yet, most schools and members of the school community are not aware of the importance of identifying the behavior and associating a threshold standard to the behavior.

Awareness of Threshold Behavior

Awareness of threshold behavior is essential if school leaders are to reduce the risk of potential violence and abusive behavior. Our awareness of events as they occur in our context lacks full comprehension. We see only a part of the picture and frequently miss entire events as they happen.

Have you ever placed your car keys down, to wonder only an hour later where you left them? Depending on the amount of time you have, you may suffer from an anxiety attack trying to locate your keys. Moments later you discover your keys and wonder how you overlooked them—after all, you searched that exact spot a half dozen times! This happens to all people. We lack awareness because our attention is diverted to another event. The event need not be real. It may be a past event or a future event that attracts our attention.

Our ability to see events, objects, or people accurately depends on our mental models. According to Senge, "Our mental models determine not only how we make sense of the world, but how we take action."[13] The more aware we are of our current reality and not focusing on past or future issues, the more we can recognize behaviors approaching the threshold limit.

ASSESSING AND MONITORING POTENTIAL AT-RISK BEHAVIOR

Risk assessment means that school leaders name at-risk behaviors or contexts. Oftentimes, educators operate from assumptions, biases, and stereotypes regarding who is at risk. Such concepts obscure the truth. The first step in assessment is to become aware of the assumptions, biases, and stereotypes that guide our actions. Our assumptions, biases, and stereotypes operate in a theory in action as opposed to an espoused theory.

Edgar Schein, MIT management expert, believes that we operate at two levels. On one level, we have an espoused theory. Our espoused theory is the way we want to act. On another level, we operate with a theory in use. Schein believes that discrepancies between espoused theories and theories in use are commonplace. For example, a school leader may claim that she treats all students equally (her espoused theory). Her actions, however, indicate something different. She ridicules students from low-income projects and refuses to invite their parents to school (her theory in use). Her espoused theory is different from her theory in use. If she operated without assumptions, she acknowledges the possibility that at-risk behavior can arise in any student, provided the right conditions exist. A second step is to use the characteristics mentioned earlier regarding each of the three types of personalities and determine a threshold for each of these behaviors. School leaders, teachers, and parents can monitor behavior and seek assistance when they recognize a student who is approaching or crossing the threshold barrier.

UNDERSTANDING THE SYNERGISTIC EFFECT OF DIVERGENT SCHOOL FORCES

Students come to school from at-risk environments. The same students may have personality characteristics that lead toward at-risk behavior. Other students, from different backgrounds, may not appear to be at risk, yet, when in a certain context, the student moves rapidly toward at-risk behavior. In essence, the school environment, including teachers, staff, and school leaders, contributes to a synergistic effect that promotes at-risk behavior. Even students who seem to operate with a set of personal controls are likely to explode and respond in unpredictable ways. Figure 8.1 shows how these forces affect a student.

The forces in Figure 8.1 represent a fraction of the total forces that each student feels. We can use an example to illustrate how the synergy of these forces creates an at-risk condition. Mark Jackson is an eleventh grade honors student at Meadowland High School. Mark's teachers consider him polite, studious, responsible, and a delight to have in class. The forces in Mark's life contribute to his success. His parents have a stable relationship and provide a loving environment to Mark

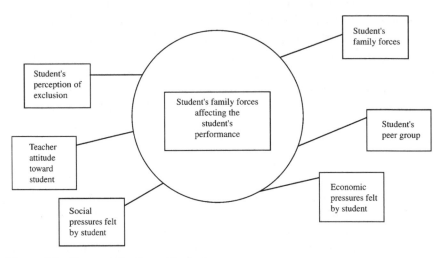

Figure 8.1 Forces Affecting a Student

and his sister. Mark does not have many friends at school, but the few he has share Mark's interests. He feels little economic pressure. His father has a professional job and provides well for Mark and his sister. Mark, although shy, started dating. He enjoys being with his girlfriend, Jennie. Mark is a part of the flow of school life. The forces in Mark's life are changing, and as these forces change, Mark's life will be dramatically affected. Mark was unaware that the idyllic life he observed at his home was coming rapidly apart. His father announced to the family that he was seeking a divorce and was moving out of the home immediately. Mark could not understand what was happening between his parents. He thought divorce happened to other kids' parents, not his. He withdrew from his peer group, and as he withdrew, they moved further away. They no longer liked Mark; he no longer was fun. Mark no longer asked his mother for money. He knew it was difficult for her to pay the bills. She had never worked out of the home. Mark grew closer to his girlfriend. She seemed to be the only person that understood Mark's problems. As Mark drew closer to Jennie, they became sexually active, and Jennie became pregnant. The day that Jennie told Mark she was pregnant, Mark had a major chemistry examination. Partially through the exam, Mark picked up his chemistry book and slammed it on the floor. His teacher demanded that Mark pick up his book. Mark refused the teacher's request. The teacher then threatened him with a zero on the exam. Mark responded by tearing up his exam and storming out of the classroom. That night Mark and Jennie committed suicide.

This story illustrates how the forces that surround us contribute to our behavior. When the forces are balanced, we feel in control and we maintain stable behavior. When the forces synergistically contribute to increased levels of stress, we see our lives as raging out of control. We react unpredictably. This can happen to any person. As a result, it is critical for school leaders and teachers to be aware of the behavior patterns of the members of the school community. When these behavior patterns approach the threshold barriers identified earlier, intervention is necessary. Otherwise, the risk to the school community increases significantly.

Another important resource that can provide additional information in constructing a risk assessment is the Web site for the Center for the Study and Prevention of Violence (http://www.colorado.edu/cspv/). The Center for the Study and Prevention of Violence (CSPV) has a panoply of information, ranging from blueprints for safe schools to fact sheets on reducing school violence. It suggests that personal and environmental characteristics combine to enhance or restrain violent behavior. Family, community, and school contexts are part of the student's environment that can enhance or prevent potential violent behavior. According to the CSPV, the contexts listed in Table 8.2 are violence-enhancing character-istics.[14] You can use this information to construct a risk assessment for your school. In Table 8.2, rate the level of existence of each of the fac-tors by placing a check mark in the appropriate column indicating the level of existence of the described behavior. You may desire to have your faculty and members of parent groups also participate in the rating so that you will gain a clear indication of the level of risk inherent in the school environment.

Table 8.2 Risk Assessment of the School and Community Context

	High Level	Moderate Level	Low Level
Family Context:			
Parents fail to set understandable expectations for their children.			
Parents ignore the supervision and monitoring of their children's behavior or peer group.			
Families have sanctions that are excessive and inconsistent.			
Families have abusive control practices.			
Families have practices that promote an unstable home environment that is violence ridden and anxiety provoking.			
Community Context:			
The community tolerates neighborhoods with high poverty and unemployment to persist.			
The community promotes the destabilization of neighborhoods by ignoring high crime rates, physical deterioration of buildings and property, and lack of resident connection to their immediate community.			
The community political system unequally distributes resources according to the political power within the community. In most cases, community resources head toward the affluent areas of the community.			
School Context:			
School officials ignore the importance of clear, understandable rules and guidelines for student behavior.			
School leaders and teachers fail to enforce rules or fail to enforce rules consistently.			
The school lacks academic focus and vision.			
School leaders and teachers ignore the importance of creating emotional support systems.			

SUMMARY

The risk environment is different in each school. Several forces determine the extent of the risk environment, many of which are beyond the influence of the school leader. The school leader, however, must be aware of these forces and develop strategies that reduce or eliminate risk. She can count on the consistency of one factor: risk increases when ignored. This chapter discussed several strategies to identify at-risk students. The school leader and her team now understand how to determine the level of risk based on the student's behavior. By identifying the level of risk, they can intervene with appropriate risk-reducing strategies.

Putting It Together: Advancing with Vigilance	✓
Prevention of violent acts is an essential component to any safe school strategy. Labeling students as at risk creates stereotypes and often misses assisting those students not labeled at risk. Labeling is a natural activity and we need to be aware of our predisposition to label. Building a sense of community is essential to lowering the risk for violence in the school. A school community needs to be inclusive. Respecting each person's viewpoint is central to building a sense of community. Dialogue is important to resolving differences and making a person feel part of a group. Be hard on the problem and soft on the person. Recognize that each student has the potential to act unpredictably. There are specific personality characteristics that indicate the potential for at-risk behavior. It is important to establish a threshold of behavior and to intervene when the threshold is reached. There are many forces at play in each person's life. These forces influence the person's behavior. A risk assessment is critical if the school is to reduce the potential for violence.	

NOTES

1. Frank Antonelli, Edward Capps, Bonnie Johnson, and Gina MacFalls, "Beyond Zero Tolerance: Alternative Strategies to Suspension and Expulsion," *The Beacon* 3, no. 2 (Spring 1999) (the Pennsylvania School Study Council, Inc.).

2. Peter Senge, *The Fifth Discipline: The Art and Practice of the Learning Organization* (New York: Doubleday, 1994).

3. Henry Levin, "Accelerating the Education of All Students," Restructuring Brief #2, North Coast Professional Development Consortium (1992), <http://cpdc.k12.ca.us/briefs/002/index.html> (10 April 2000).

4. Parker J. Palmer, *The Company of Strangers* (New York: Crossroads, 1981).

5. Roger Rosenblatt, "Welcome to the Works of the Trench Coat," *Time* 153, no. 17 (3 May 1999).

6. David Bohm, *Changing Consciousness* (San Francisco: Harper, 1991).

7. M. Scott Peck, *The Different Drum: Community and Peace Making* (New York: Touchstone, 1987).

8. Roger Fisher and William Ury, *Getting to Yes,* 2d ed. (New York: Penguin, 1991).

9. Karen Horney, *Our Inner Conflicts*, reissued ed. (New York: Norton, 1992).

10. Senge, *The Fifth Discipline.*

11. "Being Prepared," American Academy of Child & Adolescent Psychiatry (1999), <http://www.aacap.org/publications/factsfam/whenhelp.htm> (10 April 2000).

12. Judy L. Crane, "Baseline Human Health Risk Assessment: Buffalo River, New York, Area of Concern," report submitted to the Environmental Protection Agency: Great Lakes National Program Office (1993), <http://www.epa.gov/glnpo/arcs/EPA-905-R93-008/EPA-905-R93-008.html> (10 April 2000).

13. Senge, *The Fifth Discipline,* 175.

14. "Reducing School Violence," CSPV Fact Sheet, Center for the Study and Prevention of Violence (1999), <http://www.colorado.edu/cspv/factsheets/reducingschoolviolence.html> (10 April 2000).

CHAPTER NINE

Gaining Approval through Coalition Building

Even if you're on the right track, you'll still get run over if you just sit there.

—Will Rogers

The final lesson in creating and maintaining a safe school is gaining approval through coalition building. Coalition building is a political requirement for the school leader. It is through effective coalition building that the school leader and the team gain political approval for the safe school plan, sustain support during the implementation phase, and receive constructive feedback regarding the plan's effectiveness. Coalition building is the first step in implementation as the process moves from planning to action. It is through coalition building that the school leader maintains and sustains the plan. The school leader recognizes that sound plans balance the tension between flexibility and rigidity. The school leader receives feedback and shapes the plan to meet new demands.

One of the best examples of a strategic plan, adjusted over time to meet the needs of a community, is the U.S. Constitution. The planners of the Constitution prepared for change by including a process for amending the Constitution. These amendments allow the United States to adapt and adjust to evolving contexts. The safe school proposal, like the U.S. Constitution, adapts to evolving contexts by sustaining the coalition.

In this chapter, you will

- understand how to build a grassroots coalition,
- identify the barriers to a successful coalition,
- understand the process for gaining approval for the strategic safe school proposal,
- see how to launch a safe school proposal successfully, and
- identify strategies and tactics to apply to insure immediate success.

Coalition building is the final lesson in moving from planning to action. Action implies movement without hesitation. However, unguided action leads to chaos. Project managers recognize the need for directed energy if the project is to succeed. One researcher suggests that leaders follow eight principles to make a project successful:

1. Share the success of the project with all members of the school community.
2. Maintain the balance between control and delegation.
3. Balance leadership and management.
4. Make perfection a goal, but realize it is an ideal.
5. Communicate consistently and honestly with project participants.
6. Strive for simplicity.
7. Transcend the details.
8. Maintain perspective through detachment.[1]

Implementation requires constant monitoring and attention. Frequently, school leaders watch outstanding plans derail because the team's energy disappears at the completion of the planning. Implementation needs a re-birth of energy to complete the process. The rebirth of energy comes from a community-wide coalition designed to gain approval, implement the plan, and monitor the plan's progress. A successful coalition has specific characteristics:

- It is composed of a cross section of people who are actively involved in the community.
- The coalition has a clear purpose for its existence.
- The members have a singular focus tied to the coalition's goals and objectives.
- Effective coalitions have a sense of solidarity.[2]

The school leader keeps these characteristics in mind as he shapes the coalition. He always has his end goal in mind for creating a safe school environment.

COALITION BUILDING

Successful coalitions represent the entire community. The effective school leader practices the politics of inclusion and finds ways to unite members from diverse populations. Bill Smith and his colleagues in a fact sheet for the Ohio State University Extension service state, "[A coalition is] a unit composed of distinct elements of the population it serves." Given the fact that there are few, if any, populations so restricted and closed that they represent only one culture, coalition building operates on the assumption that each community has cultural diversity. As such, any coalition must represent the broad community, and the school leader has to have the ability to communicate clearly with each representative group, understand the gifts inherent in each group, and constructively manage the interactions of these groups.[3]

Successful coalition building is essential if the school leader is to gain formal sanctioned approval for the strategic safe school plan. Sanctioned approval comes through the local school district's elected school board. The school board, representing the community, provides the human and financial resources for the plan's implementation.

Timing is crucial in preparing for school board approval. When the development process begins at the start of the school year, the school team, as part of its planning process, creates a strategic approval process (see Figure 9.1). This process produces a flow of information to school community members including those in the central office and school board members. The cumulative effect of this flow of information has as its purpose to educate the community and those in authority to approve the plan as it moves its way forward for final approval. The spring is the best time to seek approval because the school leader and her team experienced a full year of planning. The leader and her team have already laid the groundwork for a successful political coalition to support the safe school plan. This year of planning affords school community members an emotional readiness for impending changes. It allows time during the summer for developing the final plans for implementation.

The school leader, through the coalition, educates those who make the final approval and those affected by the safe school plan. The effective school leader understands that widespread support is essential to the plan's success. In gaining widespread support, the school leader and his coalition establish lines of communication with the community and political approval entities. The communication process centers on answering several important questions:

- What are the purposes of the safe school plan?
- Why should the school district adopt the safe school plan?
- What changes will the safe school plan make in the short and long term?

- What can the community consider as evidence that the safe school plan is successful?
- What are the possible negative consequences of the plan?
- What, if any, contingency plans are in place?[4]

When the school leader and her team answer these questions, members of the coalition recognize that the school leader and her team are competent. A level of trust between the coalition and school leader develops. As the level of trust evolves, the coalition is more willing to take political risks for the safe school plan.

Political Approval Strategies

The effective school leader, along with his coalition, considers political strategies to ensure successful approval of the strategic safe school plan. According to Matthew Freeman of People for the American Way, there are ten strategies to follow:[5]

1. Identify those who support your program.
2. Organize your support.

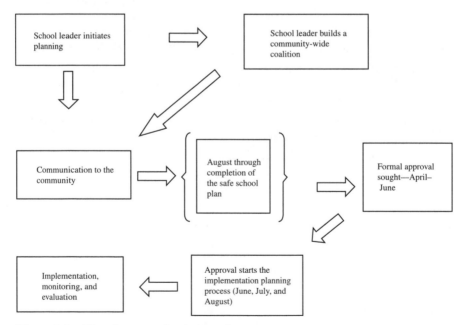

Figure 9.1   Time Sequence for Approval

3. Discover the motivation of those opposing your plan.
4. Ask for help.
5. Communicate the facts to the school community and public.
6. Avoid jargon.
7. Build support through personal contact.
8. Focus on the facts in dealing with those who do not understand your plan.
9. Build a grassroots support network before you announce your initiative.
10. Listen respectfully to opposing viewpoints.

We combine these strategies into three global concepts: (1) The effective school leader identifies and secures support of essential players in the approval process; (2) the school leader identifies legal and political questions before presenting the plan to the school board; (3) the school leader communicates with supporters and opponents, constantly seeking to educate community members to the merits of the safe school plan.

Coalition-building strategies have a single aim: to influence the vote of the school board. The school board's publicly elected members understand public opinion. The school leader is aware that "[e]very group involved in the decision process plays politics. Within each group, individuals and subgroups play internal politics to get what they want or what they see as vital to improve their organization or the human condition."[6] In effect, the school leader acts as a catalyst for coalition action.

Barriers to Successful Coalition Building

Coalition building is difficult work for the school leader. The school leader, however, who is able to build and sustain a successful coalition gains a powerful political base. The University of South Florida's Community and Family Health Program cite several barriers to the building of successful coalitions:[7]

- Turf issues
- Flawed history
- Failure to take action
- Control by professionals
- Inadequate links to the region
- Lack of organizational competence

- Leadership failure
- Lack of potential benefits for coalition members

The school leader, by understanding these barriers, uses strategies to circumvent them so that they do not derail her safe school plan. She is cognizant of turf issues. Turf issues often have a long history locked in the culture of community. In one community, for example, Pedro Sanchez, principal of Lamon High School, discovered that three different community action agencies acted in opposition to each other. These agencies often subverted each other's efforts to the detriment of the Pedro's school. Pedro brought representatives from the three agencies together to resolve turf issues. Members of the three groups could not identify the original causes for the friction. He quickly realized that these groups had a flawed history. Part of the flawed history was the domination within the groups by lawyers and social workers. Members of the neighborhood surrounding Pedro's school felt that their voices went unheeded. Pedro knew that much of the competition was professional and had little to do with community needs. He knew that these groups needed strong leadership. All three groups lacked the organizational skill to reconcile differences. If he hesitated, he knew he would lose an opportunity to unite these groups. Pedro's efforts were successful in ending the turf battle; now all three groups work together in the school's interests.

Pedro Sanchez is a politically astute school leader. He knows that coalition building is hard work. His coalition building produced benefits in terms of getting approval for much needed renovations and five additional teachers. Effective school leaders like him build broad-based support and a strong coalition from eight categories of potential supporters: teachers, parents, students, community leaders, clergy, political leaders, juvenile justice professionals, and the superintendent of schools (see Figure 9.2). Each of these groups contributes to the goals of the coalition. The effective school leader understands the political nature of coalition building and the importance of inclusionary practices to identify common ground among diverse groups.

Coalition Groups

Teachers

Teachers are important players in the development, endorsement, and implementation of the safe school strategy. The school leader needs teachers to be

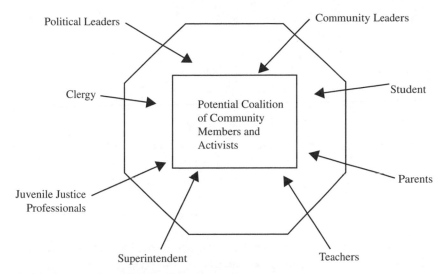

Figure 9.2   Political Coalition Groups

a part of the coalition because of the teachers' influence with students and parents, their ties to the community, and the latent power of the teacher's association or union. Teachers, as members of the coalition, can endorse the strategy as a faculty and through their representative groups. This is critical because ongoing faculty support of the plan is central to its success, and the plan must comply with labor/contract agreements. A brilliant plan that conflicts with an existing teacher contract will create opposition.

The plan, rather than generating support, serves as a lightening rod to polarize opposition. The process presented in this book, when followed, eliminates this problem by creating a partnership between the school leaders and teachers.

Parents

Parents are important to the approval process; they are a powerful political force. "Parents say they are more involved in their child's education than their own parents were, but still wish they could do more. Almost half say their child's work habits could be better. Parents also want their children to be happy and confident, and most say it's natural for parents to be less involved when kids reach high school."[8]

Parents are voters who elect the school board. The school board, in turn, is responsive to parents. Parents understand the political process and often go directly to school board members rather than to a principal or teacher.

When the school leader seeks the support of parents, the school leader recognizes that parents represent an array of racial and socioeconomic groups within the community. Since most schools have widely diverse communities, the school leader and his team build political support by involving parents from all backgrounds.

Students

Students are vital to the safe school planning and approval process since they are the primary beneficiaries of the plan. Students, as this book contends, are equal participants throughout the plan's development. High student involvement is important for several reasons. Jan Berry, executive director of Freeport West, a group treatment home for delinquent adolescent boys, states:

> There are five themes or factors that humanize institutions which are commonly mentioned by youth in our interviews with them:
>
> 1. Having choices and control over things that affect their lives;
> 2. Having a safe place to be themselves;
> 3. Being treated with dignity and respect;
> 4. Being offered relationships that create connections, connectedness;
> 5. Being surrounded by hope and promise in attitude, in the art, [and] in the opportunities for success.[9]

Student support of the proposal arises out of the students' belief that their school is a humanized institution. As students identify with their school and their part in working with teachers and administrators, their support for approval of the safe school plan will grow.

Community Leaders

Many community leaders are powerful political players. They include local and regional elected officials, business leaders, and those involved in the helping professions. These people are sociologists, social workers, psychologists, counselors, business leaders, and those in the medical profession.

John Mason, principal of Fairhaven High School, urged Martha Cannon, owner and president of Cannon Auto Sales, to speak at the school board meeting in favor of the Fairhaven High School safe school proposal. Martha is a strong political player in the community and has a great deal of influence with the community's government. Her participation in this process gained approval for the plan. Having people such as Martha Cannon speak at the school board meeting in favor of the strategic safe school plan gives the proposal credibility with the school board and community. The effective school leader identifies community leaders and seeks their advice based on the community leader's experience.

Clergy

In many communities, people closely identify with their churches. When a minister, priest, rabbi, or other religious representative endorses the strategic safe school proposal to the school board, they also endorse the proposal to their membership. School administrators often neglect the involvement of clergy because of a fear of separation of church and state. In some communities, the clergy are dominant forces in the political process.

One midwestern community's population base belonged almost entirely to one church in the community. When the superintendent of schools, who belonged to another church outside the community, proposed a policy that encouraged greater separation of church and state within the community, the school board fired the superintendent. The community wanted the existing relationship between the district and the church to continue. Although this may be a rare instance, clergy can unite people and sustain energy for a common cause. The effective school leader uses this energy to infuse the goals of his coalition.

Political Leaders

Every community has political leaders. These political leaders are city counsel members, the mayor, the city manager, state representatives, state senators, U.S. senators, U.S. representatives, and citizens elected to other political groups. These political leaders get things done. Often, influential political leaders, while no longer in an official position, retain a strong influence in the community. They can use their network of support in the school leader's coalition. The school leader involves these people by contacting them and asking for their advice on how to gain the school board's approval of the safe school proposal.

Juvenile Justice Professionals

Many students who have a history of discipline problems end up in the juvenile justice and adult justice systems. It is to everyone's benefit to find ways to lead these students to move toward a more productive social path. Once these students are in the juvenile justice system, they interact with police, juvenile judges, probation officers, and other members of the juvenile justice system. The role of juvenile justice professionals is to prevent students from entering the juvenile justice system. If students become part of the system, however, the juvenile justice professional provides guidance to help the youths return to a productive life.

Juvenile justice professionals are natural allies of the school. They are a bridge for the school leader between the school and the public. They have an interest in seeing students develop appropriate psychological and emotional restraints.

Superintendent and Central Office Bureaucrats

The superintendent's support is essential to the gaining approval of the safe school plan. Dr. John Kelly, school superintendent, states, "The active superintendent, if seen favorably in the community, will make or break a school safety plan. If it is seen as an important part of his agenda, whether he's involved directly or not, many resources will accumulate toward the goal."[10] The superintendent will make the recommendation to the school board to approve or disprove the initiative. The superintendent will approve the initiative based on the plan's merits and the political support generated for the plan. He will listen to the school leader's coalition. The superintendent, however, will resist efforts that give the appearance of bullying or subversion.

The school leader seeks the superintendent's support. She skillfully acquaints the superintendent of the plan's progress through a series of executive summaries. An *executive summary* is a one- to two-page informative report that outlines the plan at various key stages. These executive summaries give the superintendent an overview of the safe school plan. If a school board member calls the superintendent during the year and asks a question regarding the plan, the superintendent is able to offer an accurate response. Keeping the superintendent informed is an important task of the school leader.

The school leader and coalition members count votes. They know, in advance, who supports the plan or who opposes the plan. The coalition works to maintain support and to subtly increase pressure on those who oppose the plan. The school leader and her coalition subtly increase pressure through openly communicating with the public and creating widespread public support for the plan.

CONTROL OVER IMPLEMENTATION

The goal of the school leader is to have the school board endorse and approve the entire plan. Often, excellent plans derail because opponents focus on a single characteristic of the plan and make the characteristic the focal point for their opposition. The school leader and coalition are ready for this political tactic and have answers, alternative solutions, and a process of evaluation ready to demonstrate to the opposition that they will monitor and periodically evaluate the plan from its inception. The school leader has documentation related to benchmarks, expert testimony, and other alternative means of support. Attention to detail derails opposition. One way to demonstrate mastery over the implementation of the plan is to explain how the school implementation team will use a critical path analysis.

Critical Path Analysis

The implementation process can create a sense of being overwhelmed. Understanding and applying the critical path analysis (CPA) provides a measure of control over this process.

> Critical Path Analysis is an effective method of analyzing a complex project. It helps the school leader to calculate the minimum length of time for project completion and the priority of completion. Critical path analysis helps to focus attention and resources on the essential activities to complete a project. It gives an effective basis for the scheduling and monitoring of progress. The essential concept behind CPA is that some activities are dependent on other activities. For example, you should not start building a bridge unless you have designed it first![11]

Applying CPA allows the school leader to manage multiple components over time. This tool, once understood, is applicable to the implementation of the strategic safe school plan. The wise school leader can apply CPA to other complex projects using it in curriculum management, achievement testing management, budget development, project implementation, and the scheduling process.

CPA allows for sequential and parallel development of projects. Not all missions have the same sequence for completion. The effective school leader tactically gives some projects greater priority. Whenever the school leader implements a plan, she knows that consistent feedback is important in determining the plan's effectiveness. By using this process, the school leader maintains focus on specific tasks. She uses CPA to organize tasks. CPA causes those involved in the implementation to be rational and sequential. Joe Coleman, principal of Hide Park High School, for example, uses CPA to manage graduation, teacher evaluations, grade reporting, course scheduling, and budgeting. Joe stated that the use of the CPA gives him control over these major events.

CPA begins by listing every task and project that the team identifies in its proposal. The school leader links each task with a projected tentative starting date. Each task is a sequential or parallel task. A *sequential task* is one that requires completion of a previous task before initiating the next task. A *parallel task* is one in which work can start on an identified task, yet work on another task does not depend on the completion of work in progress. For example, it is important that the school leader completes the student handbook before the beginning of school. This is a sequential task. Students, teachers, and parents need to be aware of the school's rules and regulations before the start of school. A second task the school leader faces may be staff development. Staff development may start during the summer months; this is a parallel task. Staff development begins while the school leader and her team are working on the student handbook.

CPA takes on greater meaning when plotted on a chart divided into time periods (see Figure 9.3). Each time subdivision contains subdivided tasks. Each task has its initial starting date marked with an arrow through the duration of the particular project. When the school leader combines the CPA process with the benchmarking model, she has a road map to success.

In developing a CPA, the school leader overestimates the amount of time she predicts she will need to accomplish each task, knowing it is better to overestimate than to underestimate, thus creating a framework for success. She provides her team with leeway. If the team completes the task sooner, they move to other tasks. For example, suppose that the projected school board approval of the safe school plan is in August. The school board may table the motion for further study, seek clarification on certain issues, or ask for comments from people who are not present, delaying the process by a month. The effective school leader prepares for these contingencies and builds them in to her CPA.

Feedback

The final phase of the implementation plan is the five-week review. The five-week review is a call for a day of recollection among school community members: students, teachers, parents, and administrators. During this day of recollection, students and teachers react to the safe

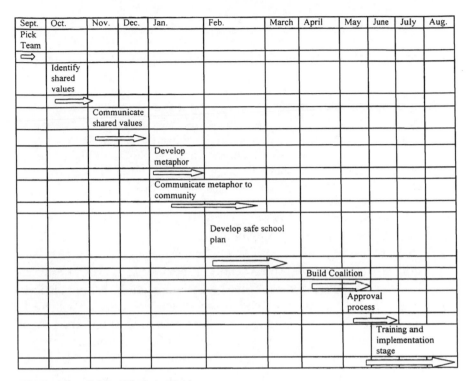

Figure 9.3   Critical Path Analysis

school plan. It is time for the school leader to gain feedback and to sustain support for the safe school plan. The school leader, at five-week intervals, reviews data to check progress toward benchmarks. During these reviews, the school leader identifies specific areas of progress, areas for continued monitoring, and areas of insignificant growth. The school leader, working with his team, establishes new goals and alternative strategies and tactics.

The school leader uses review periods to report to the school community. This report provides a status account sharing successes, struggles, and new missions and associated goals for the next five weeks. The school leader also generates a report to community leaders and the media to inform the community of the plan's progress. This builds a culture of success and support, and it demonstrates the school team's high level of commitment and competence. The school team's high performance becomes a standard for administrators, teachers, and students. It is something in which each member of the school community can take pride.

EVALUATION

The basic premise behind achieving quality is to evaluate, evaluate, and evaluate.

> Without quantifiable information, translating and evaluating the achievement of results are difficult. Information on the outcomes of processes provides the mechanism to determine the effects, either positive or negative, of changes in work processes. Measurements fulfill two fundamental needs of organizations: they assess progress as well as organizational success in meeting mission objectives and customer expectations.[12]

Through the continuous process of evaluation, the school leader moves closer to benchmarks set in the planning process.

The school leader understands that one major purpose of collecting data is to demonstrate integrity. Some school leaders make a critical error in only collecting supportive data. This is a charade, and the school leader's integrity is quickly suspect. Effective school leaders know that there is nothing to fear from data. If the safe school plan is working, the school leader uses data to verify that it is working. If there are problems, the effective school leader wants to identify the problems and apply the correct solution. Irving Janis and Leon Mann, in their seminal work, *Decision Making*, state, "Decision makers in this situation consequently remain open to the information contained in warnings and process it as objectively as they can, even though the *message is inconsistent with the course to which they are committed*" [emphasis added].[13]

The school leader uses data to make effective, quality decisions. Without appropriate data, the school leader cannot make effective decisions. A central component to ineffective decision making on the part of the school leader is his failure to collect appropriate data. Gathering appropriate data allows the school leader to consider multiple alternatives when making decisions and to move from a merely satisfying decision-making strategy to an optimizing decision-making strategy. When a school leader uses a "satisficing" strategy, he chooses the first viable alternative that appears to resolve his problem without considering other alternatives. When the school leader uses an optimizing strategy, he considers an array of alternatives, weighing their benefits, before making his final selection.

The effective school leader realizes that data provides valuable information for bolstering support. No one wants to be associated with an unsuccessful venture. People want to associate with success. When the school leader provides information that demonstrates success, those who were part of the process deepen their commitment and actively recruit others to join. According to Abraham Maslow:

> If you take into yourself something important from the world, then you yourself become important thereby. You have made yourself important thereby, as important as that which you have introjected and assimilated to yourself. At once, it matters if you die, or if you are sick, or if you can't work, etc.[14]

The school leader and his team collect data directly related to vision, mission, goals, and objectives. Although success or failure is a personal interpretation, the data provide an objective picture. Statistician Jack Levin states: "Systematically testing our ideas about the nature of social reality often demands carefully planned and executed research."[15] When the school leader and her team systematically research the efficacy of the safe school plan, the leader gains power because data provide the leader with critical information.

At a Lennor High School faculty meeting, for example, a faculty member claimed that the strategic safe school plan was not working and things were no better than last year. The principal, Marsha Adams, asked the teacher for data to support his assertions. The teacher said that students' discipline problems were the same as in previous years. Marsha had the data available to make a comparison between both years. The data showed that there was a sharp decrease in the number of referrals. She thanked the teacher for raising the issue and allowing her to share the dramatic differences resulting from the plan.

The effective gathering of data is neither complex nor confusing. It is a straightforward process. The school leader and his team use the scientific method to collect data, determine its usefulness, and draw appropriate conclusions. The effective school leader frames data gathering so that the school community understands that the proposal, *not people,* is the focus. By moving away from evaluating people to evaluating the performance of the safe school plan, the school leader creates an environment of safety and cooperation. This psychologically safe environment sustains ongoing cooperation between the education community and the wider community.

The school leader and her team generate a hypothesis related to the safe school plan. For example, "Students involved in extracurricular activities have fewer discipline referrals than students not involved in extracurricular activities" is a hypothesis the school leader can use to determine the efficacy of encouraging students to participate in extracurricular activities. Once the school leader and his team have identified appropriate hypotheses, they collect data that specifically addresses the hypotheses.

Appropriate collection of data begins by the school leader and his team defining the parameters of the data. These parameters help define time frames, groups, policies, strategies, a demographic breakdown of students by race, gender, and grade that are referenced to teachers by race, gender, and subject/grade level. Within these parameters, the school leader analyzes data for patterns, trends, and specific measurement of preset standards.

Once the school leader and her team analyze the data, she determines whether the data raised new questions. For example, if the data demonstrate that teachers refer males more frequently to the office than females, she can question the discrepancy. The analysis must raise questions if the safe school plan is to evolve to a higher quality and exceed the established benchmarks.

The school leader also uses the data to generate recommendations to improve her safe school plan. Recommendations address new goals and a new mission aligning the safe school plan with its metaphor and vision. These recommendations lead to a new and evolving mission. The new mission leads to a series of goals that become the source of motivation for the school community. A new mission, for example, may focus on increased responsibility among student-athletes. A specific goal related to this mission may be a 50 percent increase in the involvement of student-athletes in becoming big brothers and big sisters.

Data as an Educational Tool

The effective school leader uses data to educate members of the school community. When the school leader incorporates data into the community dialogue related to constructing a safe school, he moves the discussion to a neutral arena. Frequently, political discussions regarding school policy are fraught with emotion. The school leader, by moving from emotion to data, creates a different focus for his conversations with the community. The sharing of data by the school leader encourages the maintenance of the coalition.

The collected data are also an education tool. The data focus attention on specific problems, such as the number of students with drug-related offenses, and also indicate the location and type of problems. The data present a two-sided coin: on one side, the problem; on the other side, the opportunity for further creative approaches. This is one purpose of data. It serves as a focusing tool and liberates members from remaining stuck with old ways of thinking and acting.

Information, as important as it is in helping the school leader to evaluate the effectiveness of the plan, is also the source of paralysis by analysis. There comes a time in every organization where action replaces analysis. Analysis is useful and powerful when used effectively. It is like any other tool in the hands of a skilled craftsperson.

TEN HIDDEN TRAPS

The school leader must avoid ten hidden traps when developing and implementing a safe school plan:

1. Failure to recognize the change in contextual conditions in the cultural environment of the school
2. Basing safe school strategies on assumptions that have inherent flaws
3. Using a single strategy to achieve goals
4. Using strategies without a clear focus for their application
5. Failure to tag short-term goals to long-term goals
6. Failure to build a coalition to support safe school proposals
7. Failure to identify respect, dignity, and civility as priorities
8. Maintaining the belief of educator infallibility
9. Ignoring integrity
10. Importing canned programs to resolve discipline problems

Failure to Recognize the Change in Contextual Conditions in the Cultural Environment of the School

The teaching and educating culture changes at a rate different from change occurring in the community. The culture of the school frequently is out of step with the demands of society. For example, many schools in the United States have a significant number of computers. In these same schools, however, several teachers fail to incorporate the use of the computer into their teaching strategies. The computers are there, students are there, but there is little, if any, connection among the three essential elements: teacher, student, and computer.

There are demographic changes resulting in rapid demographic shifts. For example, in one transitional community, as little as five years ago, the students were from upper-middle-class and upper-class environments. Ninety-eight percent of these students went to college. This is no longer the case. This community now has a large number of students from lower socio-economic environments migrating to newly constructed apartment dwellings. The teachers, however, still teach to the culture that originally dominated the school. The teachers have not changed. This happens in many urban environments. The more aware that the school leader is of shifting contexts and environmental conditions, the more he can adjust and adapt to new demands.

Basing Safe School Strategies on Assumptions That Have Inherent Flaws

School leaders often tie their assumptions to biases and stereotypes. A safe school strategy based on the assumption that only minority members join gangs, for example, is a false assumption. A school leader who makes that assumption and directs an antigang strategy toward minorities is creating a strategy with inherent flaws. The school leader and his team must operate on accurate data and avoid making assumptions. Recognizing false assumptions provides the school leader with an opportunity to reflect on attitudes and biases that are at the core of challenges of racism, sexism, and other charges of prejudice.

Using a Single Strategy to Achieve Goals

No single strategy is appropriate to every situation. Multiple strategies and an array of tactics fitting these strategies are crucial. The effective school leader adapts each strategy to its context. For example, a strategy of communicating with parents via the Internet and e-mail may be an effective strategy in a community where many parents have computers and are on-line. In other communities where parents do not have that technology, a different type of strategy is essential. These two different environments need two different strategies.

Using Strategies without a Clear Focus for Their Application

The effective school leader is sure of what she wants to accomplish when she employs a strategy. If she uses suspension as a strategy, she already understands its purpose and place in the safe school plan. If alternative learning centers are essential, she identifies their purpose. Knowing the purpose of a strategy is crucial for the school leader. When the school leader understands the purpose, strategies have a clear purpose with intended outcome.

Failure to Tag Short-Term Goals to Long-Term Goals

It is important to link the vision, mission, goals, strategy, and tactics. Where there is no link among these items, the school leader loses consistency and flow. What exists is a random, sporadic approach to achieving a nebulous goal. The effective school leader avoids this crisis approach. The school leader's safe school goals link monthly, weekly, and daily goals. Goals eliminate waste. Goals create efficiency. Goals create success.

Failure to Build a Coalition to Support Safe School Proposals

The single most important factor in constructing a safe school is to build a coalition. Creating a strong coalition has long-range implications. The coalition helps to gain initial approval and then to generate the sustaining resources. If the school is in a high-crime area and it is difficult to monitor weapons brought to school, the school leader, with the coalition's help, acquires the technology to address the problem. Resources are critical with personnel and technology. Without the personnel to work with, counsel, and coach students and teachers, the most highly developed plans fail.

Failure to Identify Respect, Dignity, and Civility as Priorities

Respect, dignity, and civility are as important as English, math, science, and social studies. When seen in this light, respect, dignity, and civility are a cross curricula theme. A proactive response by the school leader includes respect of persons and property, personal dignity, and civility in interpersonal relationships in providing a safe, secure, healing, and nurturing environment.

Maintaining the Belief of Educator Infallibility

Effective school leaders do not assume infallibility. They know that no one has all the answers. These leaders benefit from the process defined in this book. They understand that this process empowers them to work with a wide range of people who have different perspectives. Their perspectives, experience, and knowledge base provide insights and answers vital to the success of the safe school plan. The best leaders recognize how little they know. As they become more successful, they realize that most of the solutions exist in the minds of other people.

Ignoring Integrity

One fundamental leadership characteristic is integrity. Ignoring integrity has led to the downfall of leaders and well-developed plans. Integrity implies consistency in actions driven by an ethical code. A school leader with integrity will not side with a teacher when a teacher is wrong nor will the school leader side with a powerful parent when that parent's child is wrong. Being a person of integrity is often a lonely and painful path, yet it generates respect for the school leader.

Importing Canned Programs to Resolve Discipline Problems

Canned programs have important concepts that can be adapted to a variety of contexts. The school leader, however, has to develop a safe school plan unique to his environment. It is important that the school leader is aware of programs that other people develop. These programs have important components. Nonetheless, the effective school leader analyzes these programs before adopting them. When bringing any externally developed program into a school, the effective school leader makes sure that the program conforms to his school, community culture, and the sophistication of teachers, parents, and students.

SUMMARY

This chapter involved three critical concepts: coalition building, control over implementation, and evaluation. Effective school leaders take time to plan for implementation. They take time to develop the proper strategies and tactics to ensure that their coalition and school team successfully implement and monitor their safe school plan. Evaluation is an important factor in monitoring progress. By using the data constantly to monitor progress and to motivate the school community, school leaders use evaluation as an effective educational tool. Effective school leaders are aware of the traps that exist. The traps are seductive in that they promise a quick fix and lead to reliance on intuition as opposed to quantitative data.

By now, the school leader and his team have an effective safe school plan for their school community. As the school leader, you have the tools for implementation. You can use this knowledge in developing a safe school plan with other groups and schools in your area. You are now a resource. Your school is the benchmark, and you are the leader of a benchmark school. Use it to build effective, safe schools in your area. Use it to create effective, safe communities in your area. You are on a journey that will build safe, effective, healthy schools and communities.

Internet Resources

The following are Internet resources for the school leader who seeks additional resources in coalition building and in the political process:

- The Ohio State University Extension service put together a comprehensive set of fact sheets that deal with coalition building. The fact sheets act as executive summaries. http://www.ag.ohio-state.edu/~ohioline/bc-fact/ (14 February 2000)
- Kenneth R. Bolen, director of Cooperative Extension, University of Nebraska, Institute of Agriculture and Natural Resources, *A Process for Building Coalitions: What Should You Consider in Building Coalitions?* NebGuide. http://www.ianr.unl.edu/pubs/family/g988.htm (18 April 2000)
- "Collaboration and Coalition Building" is a Power Point presentation available on the Internet that walks a person through the various steps in building a successful coalition. http://www.dmhas.state.ct.us/sig/smith/sld001.htm (18 April 2000)
- In *Building Political Power and Community Coalitions*, the AFL-CIO labor organization offers advice on building powerful political organizations. The principles used by labor organizers to develop support for labor causes are similar to the principles the school leaders applies to the political process in getting the safe school plan approved. http://www.paywatch.org/unioncity/goal3.htm (18 April 2000)

If you are able to complete the checklist on page 204, you are ready to present the safe school plan to the school board for approval. You are

Putting It Together: Advancing with Vigilance	✓
Have you recruited a broad-based coalition? Have you built a political base to assist in the approval process? Does the team understand the importance of appropriate timing? Have board members and the superintendent been kept abreast of progress in the development of the safe school plan? Are the community political leaders supporting the safe school plan? Has your safe school plan been reviewed by the state department of education? Has your safe school plan been reviewed by the district's attorney? Do you have an implementation plan? Do you have an evaluation plan for five weeks? Ten weeks? One semester? One year? Is the team aware of the potential traps?	

ready to implement and build a healthy, safe environment for teachers, students, parents, and community members. Take pride in your accomplishments!

NOTES

1. Bob Puccinelli, "Principles of a Project Leader," *Inform* 13, no. 1 (1999): 50–51.

2. Pat Bakalian, "Coalition Building How To's," *TAPII*, <http://www.hs.state.az.us/tapii/tapii0.htm> (28 June 2000).

3. Bill Smith, Ann W. Miller, Thomas Archer, and Carla Hague, "Working with Diverse Cultures," Fact Sheet CDFS-14, the Ohio State University Extension, <http://www.ag.ohio-state.edu/~ohioline/bc-fact/0014.html> (10 April 2000).

4. These questions are adapted from Ruth Conone, Donna Brown, and Russell Willis, "Understanding the Process," Fact Sheet CDFS-13, the Ohio State University Extension, <http://www.ag.ohio-state.edu/~ohioline/bc-fact/0013.html> (10 April 2000).

5. Matthew Freeman, "Ten Things to Do When the Radical Right Comes to Town," *Institute for First Amendment Studies* (1998), <http://www.berkshire.net/~ifas/fw/9511/guide.html> (12 April 2000).

6. *Decision Process Guidebook,* Bureau of Reclamation, U.S. Department of the Interior, <http://www.usbr.gov/Decision-Process/politics.htm> (10 April 2000).

7. Kelli McCormack Brown, "Barriers to Coalition Building and Strategies to Overcome Them," Community and Family Health, University of South Florida (1999), http://www.med.usf.edu/~kmbrown/Barriers_to_Coalition_Building.htm> (10 April 2000).

8. Steve Farkas, Jean Johnson, and Ann Duffett with Claire Aulicino and Joanna McHugh, "Playing Their Parts: Parents and Teachers Talk about Parental Involvement in Public Schools," *Public Agenda* (1999), <http://www.publicagenda.org/specials/parent/parent.htm> (10 April 2000).

9. Jan Berry, "Humanizing Institutions That Serve Youth," speech presented at the Giselan Konopka Special Lectureship Division of General Pediatrics and Adolescent Health, University of Minnesota (1995), <http://www.cyfc.umn.edu/Documents/I/D// ID1007.html> (28 June 2000).

10. John Kelly, Superintendent of Schools, Boerne Independent School District, Boerne, TX, per written correspondence (April 2000).

11. "Critical Path Analysis," *Mind Tools,* <http://www.demon.co.uk/mindtool/crit-path.html> (10 April 2000).

12. "Total Quality Management," *Quality Journey,* Part 3:8, U.S. Department of Energy, <http://apollo.osti.gov/html/quality/eqj3.html> (10 April 2000).

13. Irving Janis and Leon Mann, *Decision Making: A Psychological Analysis of Conflict, Choice, and Commitment* (New York: Free Press, 1997), 207.

14. Abraham Maslow with Deborah Stephens and Gary Heil, *Maslow on Management* (New York: Wiley, 1998), 10.

15. Jack Levin, *Elementary Statistics in Social Research* (New York: Harper & Row, 1997), 3.

Index

About the Author

Dr. Ray Calabrese is a professor of educational leadership at the University of Texas at San Antonio. He has significant public school administrative experience including work as an assistant principal, middle school principal, and high school principal. His middle school was recognized in a Phi Delta Kappa publication as having exemplary discipline. He is the author of three books focusing on school leadership as well as numerous articles for national and international journals.